FREEDOM TO LIVE

THE ROBERT HARTMAN STORY

Second Edition, 2013

Robert S. Hartman

Edited by Arthur R. Ellis

WIPF & STOCK · Eugene, Oregon

Wipf and Stock Publishers
199 W 8th Ave, Suite 3
Eugene, OR 97401

Freedom to Live
The Robert Hartman Story, Second Edition, 2013
By Hartman, Robert S. and Ellis, Arthur R.
Copyright©1994 Robert S. Hartman Institute
ISBN 13: 978-1-62564-500-5
Publication date 12/1/2013
Previously published by Rodopi, 1994

To Rita and
all the Hartmaniacs

(Dedication of the First Edition, 1994)

In Memory of
Bob, Rita, and Jan Hartman

(Dedication of this Second Edition, 2013)

LIST OF PHOTOGRAPHS

About the Second Edition

This Second Edition of Freedom to Live: The Robert Hartman Story includes many minor editorial improvements, a new and much expanded table of Contents, a much more detailed Index, and new photographs. Many thanks to Stacey McNutt for the new photos she contributed to this Second Edition—Numbers 1, 5, 6, and 11. Many thanks also to Rodopi, Amsterdam - New York, its original publisher, for returning the rights to this book to the Robert S. Hartman Institute.

CONTENTS

EDITORIAL FOREWORD

A complete autobiography can never be written before the author is deceased; but by then it is too late. Robert S. Hartman completed his personal/philosophical autobiography on Oct. 10, 1963, but he was to live for almost another ten eventful years, until Sept. 20, 1973. The rest of the story of his life is told by Arthur R. Ellis in the Appendix titled "Hartman's Last Ten Years" which appears at the end of this volume. Hartman's *Freedom to Live: The Robert Hartman Story* was written originally for presentation to management development seminars sponsored by Nationwide Insurance Company during 1962 and 1963 as a way of introducing businessmen to the man Robert S. Hartman and to his formal axiology. We would like to thank Mr. Lee A. Thornbury, Senior Attorney of Nationwide Insurance Company, for reviewing the manuscript and determining that Nationwide Insurance has no claim upon it.

Between 1968 and 1973, Robert S. Hartman was a research professor at the University of Tennessee. During this period, he usually taught for half a year here at U. T. and the other half was spent at the University of Mexico, where he was also a research professor. I was fortunate enough to get to know him and to sit in on a number of his classes during that period of time, and we had many lively philosophical debates. I never quite came to agree with him on every philosophical issue, but I certainly recognized that he was a philosophical genius from whom I could learn many important things. I hope that the reader of this autobiography will be able to say the same, while reserving the right to disagree where necessary, as I have always done.

In many ways, my own thinking has been more influenced by Bob Hartman after his death than during his life. More than any other philosopher, he has helped me to understand and appreciate the intrinsic value of individual persons, of unique centers of conscious experience and activity. Other philosophers have usually found intrinsic value only in universal repeatable qualities like pleasure, knowledge, virtue, the moral law, creativity, etc., not in individuals. Unfortunately, any identification of intrinsic values with repeatable universals has the effect of relegating to the status of extrinsic goods the conscious individuals in whom the universals are instantiated. In traditional ethical theories, whether they give hedonistic or pluralistic accounts of things that are intrinsically good, individual centers of consciousness are relegated to the status of extrinsically useful but intrinsically worthless receptacles into which good things like pleasure, truth, conscientiousness, the moral law, etc., can be poured and temporarily stored. Robert S. Hartman provides us with a poignant corrective to this bias toward universals and against individuals that has dominated traditional ethical theory. His theory does not diminish the capacity of universal goods to enrich our lives, so Hartman's emphasis on the intrinsic worth of individuals must be taken with utmost seriousness as a corrective to the biases inherent in traditional ethical theory. As he will show in the following pages, the whole fate of life on earth may depend on it.

Unfortunately, it is not philosophers alone who have disvalued or undervalued individuals. Many persons, especially those in positions of power and influence, are and were willing to sacrifice the well being and even the lives of individual persons for extrinsic and systemic goods. The world over, persons (and other valuable living things) are constantly being destroyed for the sake of extrinsic goods such as wealth, oil, jobs, power, territory, or social status, or for the sake of systemic goods like religious dogmas, political ideologies, ethnic purity, national sovereignty, and military glory. Robert Hartman can help us to understand the folly of these valuational perversions.

I have strongly supported and encouraged the publication of this autobiography, partly because it tells an engrossing story of the fascinating life of a person that I knew as a friend and mentor, partly because it shows how he arrived at his passionate and deeply reflective convictions about the intrinsic worth of individual persons, and partly because it shows that it is so easy to miss this essential truth in so many different ways. The consequences of doing so are disastrous for every individual and for the whole of humanity.

Arthur R. Ellis, a good and active member of the Robert S. Hartman Institute for Formal and Applied Axiology, recommended to me that we publish Hartman's autobiography and did most of the editorial work essential for its publication. I am happy that we are able to publish *Freedom to Live: The Robert Hartman Story* as the first volume in the Hartman Institute Axiological Studies series.

Arthur R. Ellis and I would like to give special thanks to Mrs. Rita Hartman for granting us permission to publish this autobiography and for supplying us with the first seven of the photographs that are reprinted at the end of this book. We would also like to thank Dr. David Mefford for supplying us with the eighth photograph of Dr. Hartman lecturing at The University of Tennessee in 1970. Finally, we express our appreciation to Houghton Mifflin Company for giving us permission to quote from Lloyd C. Douglas, *The Robe*, 1942.

This Second Edition of *Freedom to Live: The Robert Hartman Story* includes many minor editorial improvements, a new and much expanded table of Contents, a much more detailed Index, and new photographs. Many thanks to Stacey McNutt for the new photos she contributed to this Second Edition—Numbers 1, 5, 6, and 11. Many thanks also to Rodopi, Amsterdam - New York, its original publisher, for returning the rights to this book to the Robert S. Hartman Institute.

Rem B. Edwards, Lindsay Young Professor of Philosophy, Emeritus, The University of Tennessee, Knoxville, August 1993, and November 2012

PREFACE

Thirty years have elapsed since Robert S. Hartman wrote the autobiographical work which follows; yet the ideas and issues he presents, interwoven with his own life experiences, are as vibrant and vital today as they were at that time. His quest to define "good" and find ways to apply that concept to our lives is still of extreme importance to us both individually and globally. Conflicts within and between countries are occurring around the world. The use and control of nuclear capacity is still a major concern. The United States, like many other countries, is confronted with violence, drug abuse, ethical questions, environmental problems, and health care issues. Value situations requiring us to sort out the relevant in the complex are daily occurrences both in our personal lives and on the international level.

Robert Hartman's life experiences as presented in this writing are interesting and engaging. From his childhood in Germany during World War I to his young adult years when his homeland was under the influence of the Nazis from whom he had to flee, he describes the events which shaped his thinking. His background as judge, businessman, philosopher, and member of the international community contributed to the richness of his life. Seeing the Nazis "organize evil" made him wonder how to go about organizing good.

Within this volume he gives the reader an overview of his theory of value, not in great depth as in some of his other writings, but sufficiently to allow one to grasp the fundamentals. His answer to the question "what is good?" builds on the work of philosopher G. E. Moore, and his formal theory is developed from the resulting axiom. Formal axiology generates three dimensions of value: systemic, extrinsic, and intrinsic. Dr. Hartman defines these dimensions for us and demonstrates their interactions. Then he shows us how these dimensions of value apply to every area of our existence. Dr. Hartman was concerned not only with the question of what is value, but also with how to value; he believed that his method makes the process of valuation a more exact operation, introducing orderly thinking into moral subjects.

Paul Weiss, Sterling Professor of Philosophy at Yale University, said this about Hartman:

No one, I am convinced, who will allow himself to follow Dr. Hartman's relentless systematic inquiry into the nature of value will be able to free himself from the awareness that he has been engaged in a new intellectual adventure whose consequences and influences promise to be vast and varied.[1]

Freedom to Live was originally written for a series of seminars given by Dr. Hartman to the top management personnel at some of the nation's largest corporations. Their interest in his philosophy stemmed from their desire for their executives to develop more sensitivity to the human aspects of management decisions. This is of no less concern in the 1990s than it was in the 1960s.

In relation to the meaning of one's life and one's work, Hartman presents four questions for reflection:

1. What am I here for in the world?
2. Why do I work for this organization?
3. What can this organization do to help me fulfill my meaning in the world?
4. How can I help this organization help me fulfill my meaning in the world?

In the course of answering these questions we are taken on a personal exploration of the systemic, extrinsic, and intrinsic dimensions of value as they apply to our individual lives. The purpose of this exercise is to help each of us in our search for meaning and in our endeavor to prioritize our values as we make decisions. Dr. Hartman also explores our spiritual nature by applying his thinking to the intrinsic realm in religion.

Robert Hartman's vision was to give us the means to recognize and fulfill "the good" within each of us, thereby enriching our lives. By applying these principles on a broader scale, we may also enrich our world and make it a place of more "goodness" and peace. When the light of formal axiology is cast upon our world, the elements involved in making particular decisions are revealed with a kind of value clarity previously unknown.

George Kimball Plochman describes Hartman's work as follows:

Sympathy and wit counterbalance Hartman's enormous load of erudition– . . . a delighted sweep of the eye through his personal library will quickly convince one of his wide reading – and although he stresses the need for extricating scientific thinking about value from the act of valuing itself, we feel him to be directly engaged in a clear-headed reflection about the world and its goodness – and what he calls no-goodness. [2]

The concluding chapter, "The Final Years," covers the decade between the end of Hartman's manuscript and his death. It is a compilation of information from the Robert S. Hartman Collection at the Hoskins Library at the University of Tennessee at Knoxville and conversations with Mrs. Hartman and various colleagues. Interspersed are recollections from my own experiences and interactions with Dr. Hartman as my teacher, mentor, and friend.

Several people contributed to the preparation of this work for publication. I offer my thanks to Charlotte B. Ellis for editing assistance and Rem B.

Edwards for consultation and support. Rita Hartman kindly sorted through many photographs to find those used here. May Louise Zumwalt, Martha F. James, and Jane Williams contributed support and effort. My thanks to my Hartman Institute colleagues who supplied insights and pieces of information.

Dr. Hartman wrote much the same way that he spoke. An effort has been made in this text to preserve the integrity of his presentation, with changes being made only where necessary for the sake of clarity.

The message contained in this work is timeless and of infinite value to humankind. It is the legacy of a life devoted to making the world a better place to be.

Arthur B. Ellis, M.S., C.P.C.
Editor
August 1993

Chapter One

"I WAS BORN TO DIE"

On the day of my birth, January 27, 1910, the streets of Berlin were decked with bunting, the black-white-red flags of the German Empire flew from all the windows, garlands draped the house fronts, and Germany's armed might paraded through the capital's magnificent avenues to the Column of Victory with its golden angel on top.

For it was also the Emperor's birthday, the occasion for celebrating, each year, the military triumphs on which the new German Reich was built. This was the day when Kaiser Wilhelm and his six sons, each in a uniform of the various military formations, showed their faces and their power – the power of Germany – to the German people. Germany, whose imperial word was obeyed around the world, from Dares-salaam to Kiaochow, from Heligoland to Samoa, from Windhuk and Lome, Rabaul and Bougainville to Bikini and Eniwetok. All these, circling the globe, were German military bases. The world listened when the German Kaiser spoke. He was power, world power. *Deutschland, Deutschland über alles* was no vain boast.

I dimly remember the Great Parade on my fourth birthday – the gaiety, the excitement, the singing of the patriotic songs as His Majesty Wilhelm II, by the Grace of God Emperor of Germany and King of Prussia, rode gloriously through his city.

These were the wonderful days Wilhelm had promised. It was great to be alive and to be German.

But it was not until one Sunday that spring that I first consciously saw the Kaiser. Sharing a common birthday, I had pictured him as a figure of happiness. For me he was a golden knight, and the angel on top of the Column of Victory, which I had seen on walks with my parents, blended with the Emperor's person into an image of glory.

That spring Sunday I was walking with my parents in the Tiergarten. Suddenly, I heard my father shout, "The Emperor!" Amid great commotion, in a handsome carriage drawn by exquisite horses, there were passing the Emperor and his spouse, Kaiserin Auguste Viktoria. The splendor of the imperial appearance should have made a happy impression upon me, but by some trick of vision, it became an impression of terror. When I looked, there grinned at me a big skull with hollow eyes, a hole for a nose, and two crossed bones underneath.

The Kaiser was wearing his favorite uniform, that of the *Totenkopf Husaren*, the Death Head Hussars, and I happened to have looked at the huge cap, with its bushy feather topping and its skull and bones insignia, instead of the Emperor's face. This, I discovered a bit later, was quite handsome, though somewhat cold and overbearing with its stiffly upturned mustache. But from then on I shuddered at the death head insignia; to me they became the face of death. This was not so to many of my countrymen. For not only were the death head insignia worn proudly by the Emperor and his Army dignitaries, they were sold in jewelry shops and worn as decorations by girls with an aesthetic weakness for the military uniform. Years later, as I reflected upon the popularity of the insignia, it seemed to me to symbolize both the glorification and the trivialization of death in Germany. Glorification of death, I came to feel, was blasphemy against life, and trivialization was blasphemy against death.

The shock of seeing the death head atop the Kaiser in the Tiergarten was the first of four remembered experiences which by the time I was five years old had shaped my life. The second memory is of my father and mother dancing through the living room one August day in 1914 because my father had been accepted as a volunteer in the Kaiser's army. The glory of the Kaiser had entered our home. There were handshaking and congratulations all around. Germany, the greatest, the most cultured country in the world, had been attacked by her enemies, perfidious Albion, degenerate France, and brutal, backward Russia; and Germany responded as one man.

As my parents danced, so millions danced all over Germany -- in homes, streets, bars, parks, on the piers. Strangers danced with strangers and felt one in the intoxication of common greatness. They felt lifted up to an ideal, the ideal of the Fatherland. They felt the falling away of all differences, the oneness of rich and poor, of nobility and the common man, of the Kaiser and his people. They thought the war would eliminate the troubles of peace, purging away all the unclean and bringing to culmination the splendors of life. They danced for the sheer joy of adventure; they danced for what they thought was life. It turned out to be death.

Shortly after my father left for the war, not to return until it had ended, my mother took my three-year-old brother and me to Munich. In my third memory of 1914 I see myself sitting on our garden wall in Munich watching the soldiers marching to war. An endless stream of men, a river of grey uniforms, filled the wide street, and floating above it were the strains of the songs of girls and soldiers. The soldiers looked strong and happy, the flowers and green branches stuck into their helmets waved in the air, and the girls ran beside them, taking two steps for every one of the marching men, singing and crying.

I figured out what this meant, to be marching off to war. The men were going to the railroad station to be loaded on trains. The war, I thought, must be a big manhole, as in a street. The trains pulled up at the manhole, and the men jumped down from the cars and into the hole. When a man stumbled as he jumped off, he fell into the manhole, and then he had "fallen in the war," been killed.

This spectacle of marching men, with its aesthetic commotion, the songs and flowers, the flags and music, went on day after day for four years. Though it stirred me, I saw the dark side only. I remember thinking of the final destination, the helplessness of the fallen man disappearing into the black and bottomless manhole.

I didn't know why I felt that way. As far as I knew, other kids didn't. But I remember I was never able to share the enthusiasm of the cheering crowds; and military music which thrilled others did nothing for me. Neither did I feel protected by the marching men; on the contrary, I felt they needed protection worse than I. As the war went on, I seemed never to be impressed by military feats, but I was stirred when I heard and read the stories of suffering which my father wrote for the German Journal of the Trenches and sent home.

My first three experiences were harbingers of the fourth. I came to think of my first three as the Face of Death, the Dance of Death, and the March of Death. In the fourth I felt Death itself.

I remember I was standing in the downstairs hall of our house in Munich when I became conscious of a strange crying, not of a child, more like that of a grownup. I followed the sound to the third floor of the house, where my Uncle Alex, a young man of twenty-two, lived. The crying came from his room. I opened the door and there, sitting on his bed, was my uncle, half dressed and crying. I remember asking, "Uncle Alex, why are you crying?" He said, "*Ich muss in den Krieg* – I have to go to war." "Why do you have to go to war?" I asked. "*Der Kaiser befiehlt es* – the Emperor commands it." "Well," I said, "stay and don't go." And he looked at me with eyes so sad I have never forgotten them. "I can't," he said, "and I am going to die." As he said this I felt steel tongs gripping my body. A cold dread filled me. I turned and ran from the room.

I still remember my bewildered thoughts. How is it possible for the Kaiser to have the power to send my uncle to die? Does he have to go like a sheep to slaughter? A foreboding of disaster seemed to overwhelm me. The whole world seemed dark and fearful. I felt threatened and confused. I wanted to rebel. But I couldn't; I, too, was trapped, like Uncle Alex. When he had said, "*Ich muss in den Krieg*," my childish imagination had grasped the word "*Krieg*" in all its menacing double meaning. For *kriegen* in German not only means "to make war" but also "to get." Thus, it flashed through my mind, "They've got him, the Kaiser has thrown a net over him and trapped him. Unless I run away fast he'll get me, too."

Uncle Alex did die. Nobody knows where, he simply did not come back from the war. He was officially missing. He became another unknown soldier.

Reflecting upon this chilling experience today, I still feel the monstrousness of an earthly power that can send a young man of twenty-two to die. Struggling for consciousness in my youthful mind, I'm sure, was the thought that somehow something had gone wrong, somehow life and death were all mixed up, transposed. I found out fairly early that being born in Germany in the early twentieth century was dangerous, more dangerous than being born somewhere else.

I could just as well have been born somewhere else. My father's parents had emigrated from Germany to America in 1882, when my father was two years old, and had gone to San Francisco. My grandmother could not adjust to spells of foggy weather, and the family sailed back over the Atlantic and settled in London. But there the fog was worse and it interfered with my grandmother's health, so the next move took the family back to Berlin.

My mother's parents, meanwhile, had emigrated from Germany to St. Petersburg, where my grandfather did banking for the Czar. Business was good, and they were able to retire with their two daughters to Berlin. My four grandparents converged from East and West in the German capital just in time for my parents to meet and to bring me to life in the heart of Berlin, in Bendlerstrasse, the short street between the Landwehrkanal and the Tiergarten which, in the Kaiser's Germany, formed one corner of the triangle between the three war offices – the Navy, the General Staff, and the War Ministry. During my youth, after I had been taken to Munich, the three offices were merged as the Ministry of the Armed Forces at the exact place where I was born, on Bendlerstrasse.

Thus, I have felt that a metaphysical umbilical cord connected me with German history. From where I was born the threads were woven which were to snare all Europe and eventually the whole world in a net of war. So I have always loved history as a study but dreaded her as a force. She is a drama to behold, a nightmare to be caught up in.

I also inherited an interest in history from my father, who gave up his law practice when he was thirty to write, and he wrote a number of historical novels which became German best sellers. He also became one of the first motion picture writers and directors in Germany. A fanatic of creation, he left many books and many memories. I found answers to many a problem in his notes. He had a concrete imagination and could write about things and events without ever having seen or experienced them physically. I remember a novel he did about Brazil, which brought letters from Brazilian settlers asking him for advice in their problems; still, he had never been there. His wish was that Mozart's serenade *Eine kleine Nachtmusik*, a little love song, should be played at his funeral. Why a love song for funeral music? But why not? he asked. Viewed from the "other side," he said, death surely is no matter of horror, it is a matter of love, God's love. My father was a Prussian disciplinarian, in keeping with a stern, no-nonsense exterior, but I always felt very close to him; I sensed a fatherly concern and fondness which influenced me greatly, and his death in 1934 was for me a tragic, soul-stirring experience.

About my mother I remember very little. Actually, I had two mothers. My real mother divorced my father and remarried about a year after he went off to war, and we had moved to Munich. I then went to live with an aunt and uncle in a Bavarian Alpine village. For two years right after the war I lived with my paternal grandmother in Berlin, and finally, when my father remarried in 1921, I returned to Munich to live with them.

This changing family scene meant for me a diverse religious and educational upbringing. My father was Jewish, my mother was Lutheran, my stepmother was Catholic. I received both Lutheran and Catholic religious education. In the Bavarian village, as a youngster, I attended a Catholic church, helped the priest, and began to prepare myself for the life of a monk by following a self-imposed regimen of discipline and castigation. When my father came home from the war in 1918, it should have been a great day in my life, and the teacher excused me from class to meet my father outside. But I objected. I thought I must do my duty, stay in class, and wait until after school to meet my father, whom I had not seen in four years. Finally, the teacher was able to overcome my objections, I took off my hair shirt, and my father and I took a joyful walk through the village. It was indeed a wonderful occasion. But when he suggested that we must celebrate the day with some ice cream in a restaurant, I said no, I cannot eat ice cream, I must castigate myself, I cannot allow myself such pleasures. My poor father thought I had gone crazy, which in a way I suppose I had. At eight years. It proved to be, as they say, a phase. But throughout my youth – perhaps because of the subtle effect of the symbolic place and time of my birth, perhaps because of the storm of history which so soon raged over me, perhaps because of the intellectual influence of my father – I kept worrying about problems of war and peace, life and death, problems that ordinarily would not enter a boy's head.

Slowly maturing in me was the conviction -- though I could not then put it into words – that to glorify violent death, brought about by man, was to insult God, the giver of life. My life was to me a treasure of infinite value. My death should be the culmination of my life well spent and developed, the natural end of my soul's career in the flesh. Premature death, deliberately brought about, would be a great tragedy, not only for me who had to die, but for God, whose billions of years of preparation for this vessel of life would have been in vain.

I loved life more and more consciously as I grew older – the smell of the air early on a crisp morning, the colors of the trees, the beauty of the old streets, the sounds of the city, the lonely grandeur of the mountains. The great fact of my life was being born. That I was born in a particular place called Berlin and in a country called Germany came to seem incidental. Such thinking may have been due to the cosmopolitan nature of my family, but it also corresponded to a deep feeling within me that my life was a supreme gift and that I owed it only to God.

I was aware that for some reason most of my school mates, and my younger brother, too, for that matter, felt differently. Outwardly, at least, I was like them. I played soccer, I went mountain-climbing. I was good at gymnastics. I was on the school track team for the 100-meter dash. It always annoyed my brother that I could outrun him and one time, when he noticed I was neglecting my running for reading, he decided he would train and practice and beat me. So he trained, and he ran, and he challenged me to a race. I closed my books, raced him, and the result was the same as always. He never quite forgave me, and I can't say I blame him.

I had fun running, climbing, and playing, but my first love always was for books. When I was six years old, my Aunt Henny Lux gave me a Latin-German dictionary for my birthday. I still have it. It was the start of a library which now numbers some twenty thousand volumes. When I was twelve, I bought my first book – Simon Newcomb's *Astronomy for Everybody*. It, too, has an honored place on my shelves, along with the tenth book of my library, Bruno H. Burgel's *On Far Off Worlds*, a Christmas present from my father in 1922.

In the two years after the war when I was living at my grandmother's, she and I read together *Faust* and other works by Goethe – a German who had grown into humanity. My grandmother, an offshoot of the Felix Mendelssohn family, was a bit set in her ways and she liked to smoke cigars, but she was an ardent Goethe fan. When I was ten, she took me on a Goethe tour, visiting his garden house, his palace, and all the places around Weimar where he had worked and lived. She had a wonderful time, and so did I. No wonder that in high school I played Mephistopheles in *Faust*. When my grandmother was 75, she wrote a little manuscript entitled *The Mothers: An Interpretation of Goethe's Faust* to mark the centennial of Goethe's death.

Though I had my nose in a book every chance I got – I remember smuggling a flashlight into my room so I could break the "no reading in bed" rule – I don't believe I was regarded as a bookworm. Perhaps my physical abilities saved me from that label. Anyway, my classmates elected me class president in both grade school and *gymnasium* (equivalent to high school and junior college).

With love for books went a love for other cultural experiences. In Munich there were *two* opera houses, and as a teenager I was many times a *statistic* – a waiter in *La Traviata*, a servant in *Der Rosenkavalier*, one of the chorus in *Carmen*, a gypsy in *Il Trovatore*. For these roles I got to hear the opera and made ten marks besides.

Every Sunday, our family went to an art gallery or museum, and on each preceding Saturday evening my father would read from a huge *History of Art* about the paintings we would see the next day. This was torture to my brother, who was mechanically, not culturally, inclined, but much pleasure for me.

Reading inevitably led me from one interest to another. For one thing, it enabled me to do a lot of tutoring, and with the money I bought more books. It set me off on a serious study of astronomy which years later (in 1942) culminated in an essay published in *Philosophy of Science*, "Prime Number and Cosmical Number," which demonstrated a theorem for the conformity of mathematics and physics. Astronomy continues to be fascinating to me, and I still have a powerful telescope which I wheel out on the patio in Cuernavaca on clear Mexican nights to look at constellations, the ring of Saturn, and the moons of Jupiter.

Something started me off on photography in the last few years of high school, and I won a number of prizes in school and newspaper contests. This photographic skill came in handy later on; in fact it was about all that stood between me and some very hungry days and nights in Paris.

Despite these other interests and hobbies, I kept coming back to thoughts that never seemed to enter the heads of the other kids. To them the opposite of life was not to be dead but to be non-German. To be alive meant to be German, and to die was a German matter. I became fully conscious of this difference in outlook one day at school when I was about fifteen. Every day during a certain period one of my teachers – a gentleman of the old imperial school, obviously – required us to stand up at the beginning of class and repeat in chorus a kind of loyalty oath: "I was born to die for Germany." One day, when we had intoned the formula, it struck me that the oath was false. As the others sat down I remained standing and said: "Sir, I think I was born to live for Germany." The teacher looked at me with mixed curiosity and disgust, as one looks at a repulsive but interesting bug, and then asked me to justify my peculiar statement in an essay.

I got a high mark for this paper, but the teacher never discussed it with me. Nor did he discuss with me another essay I wrote – on capital punishment – asserting that the state has no right to take a human life. This was a matter for Divine Law, I argued. In the margin the teacher wrote, "Then we should not be allowed to exterminate bedbugs, either." I wrote underneath his note, "No, in the bedbug state, we should not," and handed the paper back. But that was the end of it.

Thus, though I was able, in *gymnasium*, to make my point on the infinite value of a human life and on the moral obligation of the state to keep violent hands off that life, it bothered me that I could not prove it as I could prove the Pythagorean theorem or that two plus two equals four. I could prove these mathematical facts because of what I knew of the sciences of arithmetic and geometry, but I knew of no science from whose premises it followed that a life is of infinite value.

I reflected often about my four early introductions to death, about the countless wartime agonies and tragedies, the millions of men who died violent deaths – and it seemed to me they had died for nothing. At that stage, I blamed war and its cheapening of human life entirely upon the Kaiser and his system.

Uncle Alex, I concluded, was in 1914 one of the few who, whether he knew it or not, saw the war in human, not military, terms. He was only a simple lad who wanted to live, for he was very young, and he was not sophisticated enough to use the rationalizations which make war imperative and glorious. He was just one more innocent victim of an age in which birth, to the state, was primarily a military matter. A girl, in Germany, had been expected to be a *Soldatenmutter*, a soldier's mother, and an obscene but popular rhyme encouraged the German maiden to spread her legs for the Emperor needed soldiers.

I, too, was born as a potential soldier who would be expected to die for the Kaiser. My birth, a cosmic event for the universe, an existential event for me, a blissful event for my parents, was a military event for Germany. It was manpower, a particle of the collective power of the nation. Thus, life was reduced to a matter of military supply. Love was reduced to the biological function of mating; happiness at the birth of a baby became satisfaction at the addition of war material; and death became a statistic.

This reduction of the vital to the mechanical was implicit rather than explicit in imperial Germany. It was to become explicit in Hitler's Germany. Mating became in Hitler's Reich a regulated affair, from the Nuremberg laws on racial purity to the official "mating courts." And death became a matter of extermination with anti-vermin gas.

So it was that I thought hard and long as I neared the time when I would graduate from *gymnasium* – at seventeen – and would have to decide what I would do in life. Since I believed war to be madness, I reasoned that peace must be rationality. So I rejected all violent creeds, whether of Communism, Nazism, or Fascism. All these, I thought, belonged in the category of irrationality and violence. On the other hand, I had to admit that to say war is madness does not explain it. For the problem of war is a complex of hundreds of fragments; I resolved I would one day try to fit the pieces together into a coherent picture. The key, I decided, lay somewhere in the correct answer to the question, "Why does a killer in war get a medal and in peace the electric chair?" In my diary I wrote on May 17, 1927:

I have seen something remarkable. I was just in the movie and in the news there appeared Von Hindenburg. The people applauded. It seems people must always be enthusiastic for something. We must be careful not to direct this hunger for enthusiasm toward the military. But there must be *some* direction.

I began to put some pretty tough questions to myself. What is the value of a human life? What is the relation of that life to the state, and to God, whence it came? What is the relation of life to death? Does the state have any right to take a life which belongs to God? Is my life nothing but a chip, a token for the rulers of the state? Or am I an issue of creation, a totality, albeit a tiny one, of the universe? Am I, ultimately, born for the state, which will claim my life whenever a political ruler or a diplomat makes a fatal mistake, or for God who will claim me in His own good time? Is God truth, or is the military state truth? Some people, it occurred to me, had unwittingly chosen the military state as the higher power, the greater value. Others sought to serve two masters, both God and the military state. A number of individuals – though not many – had chosen God as the Supreme Power and defied the military state.

These questions were not (and are not) easy to answer. There is, for example, the contention of the military state that it is God-made. Its existence is "by the Grace of God," "under God," "with God, *Gott mit uns*." Is there a difference between the state and God or is there not? If there is, then my duties toward each may clash, and I will have to choose between the two. Since, as a rational person, I am morally responsible for my actions, I cannot take anybody's word in a question of such ultimate concern. It must be my duty to decide for myself. This meant I would have to find out all I could about the state, about man, and about God. Later, as I proceeded with that agonizing search, I learned I would also have to find out about my self, my inner Self.

For the time being, I tried to simplify the matter. I asked myself what is the relative value of being born and of being a German, a national. I am born by love and I am a national by law. Whether you are a national or a foreigner depends upon the accident of birthplace. I could just as well have been born a Russian, an Englishman, or an American. For the state to value the nonessential accident of birthplace higher than the essential of birth itself, one's life, seemed to me degrading and undignified. It seemed to me that I was born to live for humanity, that the importance of being born was that and nothing else. Whatever I would achieve in life – do for humanity – I would do through development of the talents and abilities given me at birth. Sure enough the civilian sectors of the state would help me along, not only the schools and universities, but all sectors, from the drainage system to the transportation, utilities, and communication systems. This civilian society, in turn, had a claim upon my loyalty and my faculties; it joined me to the rest of mankind.

For the civil state I had affection. I saw it as the sum total of all the men, women, and children, the houses, businesses, factories and organizations, the nature that gave it sustenance, the fauna and flora of the country, all that which lived naturally and under God's laws in the land which happened to be called Germany. After all, what was "my country"? Was it the castles and palaces of Berlin, the flags and passports, the military and its trimmings and trappings, the entire military apparatus of the state in relation to other states, the place from which the boots of soldiers, the machines of destruction, and the other horrors of war had gone forth into the world? Or was it the pulsating life of 65 million men and women going about their daily business in the eternal rhythm of living, a country from which light and culture had gone forth into the world? Once I was on the night train from Munich to Berlin and, looking out the window, saw a star blinking far away through the darkness. The train was moving at eighty miles an hour, but the star was not moving at all, and its distance to me did not change. The universe was an indifferent spectator, and this discouraged me. I remember awakening sadly in the morning. The train pulled into Anhalter Station and I walked out into the street, up Koeniggraetzer Strasse to the Potsdamerplatz, when suddenly the whole wave of the morning life of the city – hurrying people, impatient vehicles, calls of vendors, the rumbling and tinkling of street cars – surged toward me and swept me up. It filled me with a great lust for life. I thought to work for this city, for this people, for this world had enough meaning, if rightly done, even for the universe looking upon us so placidly and remotely.

This was the true Berlin, the true Germany, I thought, for it was the Berlin and the Germany of life. I loved it and would, in a given case, die for it, as I would die to save a drowning child, to rescue a person assaulted by a criminal, or to save the victims of a fire. These, I felt sure, are ways in which one may die for life.

But can I, who am loved and who loves, disregard the grief, the despair of the human heart deliberately arranged by and for political power? Can I barter compassion for my fellow man for a mess of collective glory? Is not the choice, again, between truth and falsity, reality and fake? For the glory of the military state, won with the deaths of millions of men, women and children, is not my glory. To attribute it to myself is the fallacy of dividing the properties of a collective among its members. Examples of this fallacy are given in every logic textbook: "Men are numerous; Socrates is a man; therefore Socrates is numerous." "The crowd is dense; John is a member of the crowd: therefore John is dense." In these examples the reasoning is obviously fallacious. But "Germany is powerful; I am a German; therefore I am powerful" was not obviously fallacious to Germans. Because Germany was militarily powerful in 1914, every German worker or mailman thought he was powerful. His pride of nationalism was based on a fake. He borrowed the splendor of the Kaiser and found it reflected in the shining buttons of his uniform. He bathed in the glory of the military spectacles which his rulers staged. He confused fact and fiction, and he forfeited his individual life and all of mind, body, and spirit that the life contained.

It seemed to me that as a German national I would have to limit the brotherhood of men to a small circle. I would have to see and think collectively. In collective terms, deaths are statistical, not human; "losses" are recoverable; troops are replaceable. Numbers alone count. Early in the war a Berlin newspaper editorialized: "We still remain a people of 65 million; a hundred thousand corpses more or less matter nothing." Germany lost in the First World War 1,808,545 dead, or three percent of her population. After the war the birth rate made up for this loss in 6.4 years. Thus, it could be argued from a collective viewpoint, Germany lost nothing. But the individual casualty was a man, loved and loving, and his loss was irreplaceable. It was a life lost, a life wasted, dumped into a manhole. The state takes human life supposedly to protect the whole. But is a human life of less value than a collective? Perhaps, I thought, in the true scale of values, the individual loss weighs more heavily than the supposed gain of the state. Perhaps the individual in his concreteness is worth more than the collective in its abstraction. Perhaps the simple arithmetic of population statistics is morally, and hence truly, false.

I felt it to be so. I did not feel like a cipher, but I did not know where the mistake lay. Again, I did not then have the intellectual tools to prove the fallacy of numbers when applied to human beings. All I could see was that there were two sides to everything I experienced, the national and the human, and that I took the side of the human when the two collided.

The more I wrestled with these thoughts the more it became clear to me that Uncle Alex had not died for Germany but for the military system and its Supreme Commander, the Kaiser. He had died for the Kaiser's folly in not foreseeing the disastrous results of his play for power, and he had died in vain. This to me was the crime of crimes, to throw onto the rubbish heap a life given by God, a life which in the giving must have included an obligation for the receiver to make the most of it.

I was deeply thankful for the lesson which I thought the German people had learned from the war. I wrote in my
diary on January 6, 1929:

I have an urge to put down in writing that I was born at a time when the picture of Kaiser Wilhelm II was adored in German households. This fact, together with the guts which hang on it, the blown-up submarines, the fried tank drivers, is so monstrous to me that not even on black and white do I feel I can understand it. Thank God we have lost the war and this system.

I did not then see that the German military system was not dead at all, that it was still virulent, still strong enough to scatter death over the globe.

At that very moment Adolf Hitler was sowing new seeds of racial hatred, inhumanity, and militarism in my country. I first saw Hitler in Munich in 1924 at his trial for attempting to overthrow the provincial government of Bavaria in the Beer Hall Putsch. With several schoolmates, I skipped classes to attend the trial. We were all impressed, for Hitler with his oratory seemed to turn the tables on his prosecutors; he appeared to be prosecuting the government of Bavaria for economic crimes against the unhappy Bavarian people rather than defending himself against the crime of treason. And he was let off with a five-year prison sentence, with eligibility for parole after six months. He was released after nine months, during which he had written most of *Mein Kampf*.

At that time I was not, of course, aware of the full import of the Nazi movement. I knew of the National Socialist clubs, which were recruiting young and old alike. Indeed, a club was organized at my school. When I was invited to meetings from time to time I learned what was going on -- the club was as much for homosexual as for political purposes. It was with some amazement, then, that in the next years I began first to fear and then to know that this psychopathic monstrosity was developing into a potent political movement.

I felt that I must do all I could to stop this growth. I began to learn all I could about political science and law. Law, I thought, would show me what was right and wrong; it would help me organize good as the Nazis were organizing evil. After finishing *gymnasium* in 1926 (we had moved from Munich to Berlin in 1925), I attended the German College of Political Science for a year, studied law at the University of Paris for another year, and for still another year attended the London School of Economics and Political Science. I returned to Germany in 1929 and got my Bachelor of Laws degree from the University of Berlin in 1932. I became an assistant county court judge and an assistant district court judge, and at the same time taught administrative law and the philosophy of law at the University of Berlin.

With intellectual tools acquired at universities in three countries, I tried to help sweep back the Nazi tide. As an assistant judge in the Beeskow district of the Mark, I imposed as severe fines as I could on Nazi rowdies who were attempting to terrorize the people with bomb blasts, beatings, window breaking, and other property damage violence. One summer evening, at the conclusion of a Nazi public meeting, I lost my head and arose angrily to denounce their movement. I didn't get far before a gang of Brownshirts tossed me bodily through an open window. From 1929 to 1932 I spoke regularly at rallies of the strong Social Democrat party and wrote many anti-Nazi articles for *Das Freie Wort – The Free Word –* the party's widely-circulated weekly organ.

In September, 1932, I wrote an article called *Die Frau Hitler –* "The Woman Hitler" – in which I charged that the Nazi leadership was dominated by homosexuals. I concluded: "The Nazi movement has not only mobilized all the stupidity in Germany, but all its evil instincts, all its political ugliness."

Shortly after *Die Frau Hitler* came out, I started work on a paper which was to lead me to a crashing fall, right through the surface of my being, and it all but finished me. The paper was to be delivered before a faculty seminar at the University of Berlin on "The State and the Political Parties." I devoted most of my time to the preparation of the paper, and found myself being driven on and on, getting in deeper and deeper as I wrestled, not just with the state and political parties, but also with life and death, war and peace, the One and the Many, and finally God, because once you start and do not stop you eventually must come to the problem of God. I felt driven to prove beyond doubt the beliefs which had piled up in me in somewhat bewildering fashion throughout my youth.

I started to put my thoughts down on paper one Sunday. There followed seven terrible days of frenzy, frustration, and horror. Strangely, in view of what happened to me, I feel as though I still remember every minute of that awful week.

My family went to see my grandmother that Sunday, December twelfth. We walked, but I lagged behind and arrived a half hour later than the others. I sat in a corner of the room with pencil and paper, worked on my manuscript, and rudely rejected efforts to involve me in the conversation. I said I didn't want to waste my time with idle talk because I had something more important to do. When my father suggested that the relation of political parties to the state was not, after all, that important, I said that one day there would be no more parties, just the state – and then what? Moreover, I said, the whole problem was much deeper. The party was just a part of the state, and the problem was really that of the relation between the parts and the whole.

At home that night, I was still sitting at my desk when my father came into the room and told me it was midnight and time to go to bed. "Yes, yes,"

I said. At three o'clock in the morning my father again came into my room. I was still sitting at my desk, writing. My father insisted that I go to bed, and I promised I would. At seven in the morning my father came in again. I was in bed, but the light was on and I was writing. I wrote all Monday, and could not be persuaded to join the family for breakfast, lunch or supper. Food placed on my desk went untouched. I kept writing. I wrote all night from Monday to Tuesday and all day Tuesday, without taking a bite and becoming more and more surly when I was asked to attend to my daily duties. I had many appointments but didn't keep them. I didn't answer calls or even dress or wash. I wrote all through the night from Tuesday to Wednesday. On Wednesday my father came into my room, sat down at my desk, and asked me about my paper.

I said I was working on a large scheme of the world embracing everything from electrons and protons, the smallest particles of matter; to the atom, which is a composition of protons and electrons; the molecule, which is a composition of atoms; and the cell, which is a composition of molecules; to man, who is a composition of cells; to the state or nation, which is a composition of men; and so on to the continent, the solar system, the galaxy, and the Universe. The whole world, I said, is one, even though it consists of these innumerable parts. My father remarked that I had not kept to my theme, "The Political Parties and the State." I answered that that problem could be solved only by solving the problem of the one and the many.

My father said later he was somehow awed by the scope of my thoughts and so let me go on, writing all night from Wednesday to Thursday and all Thursday to Friday. He only tried to make me eat a bite now and then and to talk to me about my writing. He said I kept talking about the one and how it could best be expressed as the number 1 which, like the one universe, could be divided into as many fractions as could be calculated. I said I was now calculating some general laws of atoms, molecules, stars, men, and nations, and had found a mathematical theorem that connected fractions with geometric lines. Recalling this conversation, my father said he didn't understand much of what I said and had the feeling I didn't understand much of it myself. Still, he let me go on.

That Friday night was climactic. Worrying about me, my father slept lightly. Some time in the night he heard my step outside his door, and he waited for me to knock. I did not, so he got up and opened the door. There I was in the dark corridor, he told me later, shaking heavily, my hair wet, my eyes staring glassily. I said, "I am frightened; I have seen God." "Such things can happen," my father said, and suggested that I sleep in his room. I said, "No, I must not sleep; I just want you to be near me."

My father went with me when I went back to my desk. I had written on small papers, strips of cardboard, sheets of toilet tissue, and any other white surface I could find. I explained that my thoughts had come so fast that I had no time to look for proper paper, so took anything that came to hand. My father said it would be better to take my time and write in order. And I answered testily, "I don't write; I am being written."

He said later he could make little sense of most of the writing. One phrase read: "It must be horrible to be God. God is horror. Blind me, blind me again!" I'm not sure I know why I wrote that. That was one of the papers I burned because I couldn't stand the sight of them any more. But let me speculate a bit. When we look at something from a distance, might we not consider it horrible, whereas from close up we might see that it is glorious? As the viewpoint and the relationship changes, might not horror, like hate, turn to love? When I had reached the bottom of my thoughts, I found blackness, chaos, helplessness. Somehow I connected it with God, just how and why I don't know any more. But He appeared to me horrible beyond description. It must have been for me, I think, what others have called "the dark night of the soul," the *mysterium tremendum.*

My father again asked me to come to his room to sleep, but I refused because I said I did not want to forget. I wanted to get everything down. So he stayed with me until morning and I kept on writing. Now it was Saturday and I wrote all Saturday and all night from Saturday to Sunday. That was as far as my body would go with me. I collapsed. I could not write. I could not speak. I could not see. I could hardly move, and I had a high fever. So I was put to bed. Someone fed me some apple sauce. Then the doctor came. I said to him: "In this moment a new world is born." What I think I meant was that I had caught a glimpse of a new world of harmony and values, a world of horror perhaps but also of love and pity, a true world of the spirit. In any event the doctor replied matter-of-factly: "Young man, you have had a nervous breakdown." "A nervous breakdown," I repeated, "that's a good term." I cannot describe my relief when I heard those words, "nervous breakdown." There it was. Just an illness. No divine revelation or anything like that. It made me feel on secure ground again; it was a plank to hold fast to. For a nervous breakdown is a definite palpable thing, a familiar phenomenon, and it can be dealt with in a familiar and experienced manner.

The doctor explained to my parents that I had a dangerous inflammation of the brain brought on by too much and too prolonged mental excitement. He said he was not sure whether I could be saved or whether, if I did live, I would be sane. He had this word of consolation: "If he does recover, it's unlikely such a breakdown will ever recur."

I was taken to Berlin's Charity Hospital the next day and there, for nearly six months, I struggled to climb up from the depths of nothingness to sanity, to sight, and to life. Slowly, sometimes advancing, sometimes slipping back, I made the ascent successfully. It had been a shattering experience. I had tried to stuff a lifetime of thought into one week. And it all began, I reflected afterward, with just a little curiosity. I was like a child playing at the shore, and touching a little water and wanting to touch a little more, and wading in a little, little more, until suddenly I was engulfed by towering waves and, struggle as I might, I could not come up for air. It was horrible. It was a whirling chaos, but perhaps it was also, for me, the beginning of order. It was the bottom of my life, but perhaps it was also the root of my life. When I was taken to my hospital bed, I had heard the doctor tell me, "You've lost your balance." He was right. My mind had overwhelmed my body, and all but crushed my spirit. As I emerged from darkness into the daylight of health, I began for the first time to see my life whole – and in balance. For the first time my life began to take on meaning.

On January 30, 1933, less than two months after I entered the hospital, Adolf Hitler became chancellor of Germany. When I returned home in May, I learned that the Nazis, reacting to my articles and speeches, had been to the house looking for me. Fortunately, they had not yet organized their terror efficiently and by the time I came home from the hospital they had temporarily forgotten about me.

Nevertheless, the time had come to decide whether to leave Germany, as it had come to millions of other Germans through the harrowing and bloody years until 1944. It was a decision that encompassed all the questions I had asked myself on the relative values of the state and human life, beginning with the bedbug essay and ending with the week of frenetic writing.

I had recognized and described the potential evil in Hitler for years before 1933, but even so the decision to resign from the German state was difficult. I could stay and "die for Germany." But this would not mean to die for "my" Germany, the people and their lives, the rivers and valleys, the woods and sea coasts, the cities and villages, the whole vibrant country. No, it would mean to die for the political and military rulers of Germany, just as my Uncle Alex died for the Emperor.

For eight days I took walks through the woods near my suburban Berlin home trying to decide what I should do. Was I perhaps wrong about Hitler and were many millions of Germans right, or vice versa? Would Hitler lead Germany to new peaks of world leadership or would he, like the Kaiser, lead her to tragedy and ruin? I decided I had no doubt that if this man with his tremendous capacity for hate, violence, and mendacity could organize 65 million Germans into a military organization, as he vowed to do, then there would be another world war. What was worse, the Nazis might win the war and really become masters of the world in fulfillment of their slogan – "Today we own Germany, tomorrow the whole world."

Here in Hitler's Germany, I concluded, is the very core of evil. Already he has taken over Germany. Something must be done to prevent him from taking over and poisoning the minds of all mankind.

I thought to myself, if evil can be organized so efficiently, why cannot good? Is there any reason for efficiency to be monopolized by the forces for evil in the world? Why is it so difficult to organize good? Why have good people in history never seemed to have had as much power as bad people? I decided I would try to find out why and devote my life to doing something about It.

This settled it. It meant I would have to leave the country, for in Nazi Germany I was a marked man and could do little or nothing. As soon as I had the money, I would go to America. There, I thought, would be the most fertile ground for the organization of goodness, for America, to me, was the prototype of a civilian society, with a minimum of military apparatus. My grandmother had told me that in the United States the military did not count for much. Soldiers on leave, she said, quickly took off their uniforms. They preferred civilian clothes. To be sure, like all states, America assumed power over the life and death of her citizens in case of a threat to her sovereignty. But Germany was a greater danger to her citizens because the military had penetrated further into the web of life. America, I realized, was not immune to the military virus; she could conceivably go the way of Germany, but I felt she could never confuse human values to the point of becoming *militarized*. If ever she would be, I knew, the delusion would be even more difficult to detect than in Germany, for America was born to be a world power, and militarism thus might fit her as a glove a hand. All this, however, I dismissed from my mind. As soon as I could get there, free America would be my country. I would leave Germany as soon as possible.

Those who decided otherwise were claimed body and soul by the Nazi military state, and those who resisted in efforts to remain true to the real Germany paid for their loyalty strung up on piano wires. Those of us who fled were spared the martyrdom, but in our hearts we lived through the agony, the death of the good, and the triumph of the bad. Hitler's evil was monumental: six million murders in concentration camps in six years by a hundred thousand murderers for a grand total of more than fifty million dead[3] in the war and in torture chambers, every death a hell of agony.

Among my Social Democrat friends I passed the word that I was planning to leave. One evening early in June a number of us were gathered around a big wooden table in the smoke filled corner of a beer hall. In the middle of the table was a pile of passports, obtained by one means or another for would-be refugees. Someone reached over, pulled one of the passports out of the pile, and said: "Here's one for a Robert Hartman. Anyone want to use it?" "I'll take that one," I said, and that's how I was able to get out of Germany. You see, my real name was Robert Schirokauer. That next winter, in London, chiefly to hamper the Nazis in their efforts to keep track of me, I changed my name legally to Robert S. (for Schirokauer) Hartman.

I left Germany for Paris on June 6, 1933, with only about sixty marks and a Leica camera, and it was miserable living for awhile. The money lasted only a week, and Paris can be cruel to a man who is down. One time, discouraged, I decided my family was right – I *was* crazy – and made up my mind to go back. I was actually on the Berlin train. When the conductor called the French for "All aboard!", however, I shot up from my seat and out of the car. It was a close call.

Then my Leica saved me. I had taken a picture of a Paris boulevard scene, and one of my fellow refugees was inspired to try to sell it to a Paris newspaper. I was amazed to learn that the paper had bought it. This bit of luck eventually led to the setting up of a photographic agency, *Agence Centrale*, which sold pictures to news syndicates. That December I went to London and tried to set up an English branch of the agency. But the income was meager, and I couldn't even afford pennies for the gas grate meter. I had to go to bed to get warm. And I can remember making a point of passing by bakeries just to be able to smell the bread. One minor miracle after another, though, kept me going, and one bright day in May, 1934, came a break. On a routine photographic trip to the opening of the London Air Post Exhibition, I met Gerhard Zucker, a young German of 34 who had invented a rocket, the forerunner of the lethal German V-2 rockets of World War II and of the rockets of today which are taking man into space. Zucker wanted his rocket to be used to carry mail. Hitler, he said, had wanted to use the rocket to deliver bombs, and he wouldn't go along with that, so he got out of the country. He planned to interest the British government in his rocket, and that's why he had set up a display at the Air Post Exhibition. I liked the guy, and he liked me, and I agreed to serve as his publicity man. Zucker, meanwhile, had obtained financial support from a postage stamp collection dealer named C. H. Dombrowski, who stood to gross several thousand dollars if the rocket venture turned out successfully.

The project, however, met many obstacles. Only in Germany was the proper rocket fuel produced, and the Nazis had banned its export. The cartridges had to be specially made, and no one in England knew how to pack the powder properly. The rocket runners also required a special lubricant which was not available in England. Efforts to elude the Nazi export ban, including a trip to Germany by Mrs. Dombrowski to bring fuel back in her hat box, failed. The vigilant eye of the Gestapo was watching every step taken by Zucker, as well as by Dombrowski and me. So substitute fuel (much less powerful), substitute cartridges (packed inexpertly), and substitute lubricant (butter) had to be used, and Zucker had to rebuild the rocket to accommodate the substitute materials. With German stubbornness, however, he plodded on. Finally, everything was set for the first trial. In the early morning of June 6, 1934, six men -- Zucker, Dombrowski, a reporter and a photographer from the *London Daily Express*, a philatelic magazine editor, and I – assembled secretly on a Sussex Downs hilltop. And, by golly, it worked! Three times, twice loaded with letters, the rocket flew for distances of a half-mile to a mile. The *London Express* next day had a big front page banner, FIRST BRITISH ROCKET MAIL, and a sub-headline, "Syndicate Plans 1-Minute Postal Service Between Dover and Calais."

Now the government was interested, and a public demonstration was arranged. Zucker was to fire his rocket from the Isle of Harris in the Hebrides over one mile of water separating Harris from the Isle of Scarp. Government officials were present. It was to be the first over-water rocket flight ever tried. Alas, this time it was a failure. The rocket exploded and some 1,200 letters with rocket mail stamps affixed flew all over the beach. "It was the cartridge," Zucker explained. "The powder had not been properly packed and air pockets caused the explosion."

Zucker tried again and successfully fired a rocket in December, 1934, but the blast on the Isle of Harris had killed official interest in the rocket, and Zucker could never regain the lost ground. Meanwhile, his visa had expired and he had to return to Germany. He was arrested when he stepped off the train in Cologne and put in a concentration camp. He was threatened with death unless he cooperated in developing the rocket. He refused. One day there was a small notice in the *Hamburg Fremdenblatt*: Gerhard Zucker has been executed for "an attempt to sell an invention important for Germany to a foreign power." Even so, he may have held back the development of the German rocket long enough to save many thousands of English lives in World War II. It was two more years before a rocket equal to Zucker's was produced in Germany.

In London, meanwhile, I had come across a man I thought might somehow make it possible for me to go to America one day. He was an American (typical, I thought, because he sat with his feet up on his desk) who represented Walt Disney in England. I kept pestering him until one September day in 1934 I coaxed out of him the job of representing Disney (handling licensing arrangements and contracts) in Scandinavia, with headquarters in Copenhagen.

It was shortly after I had set up shop in Copenhagen that my father died. I had not seen him since I left Germany for Paris, and he had gone to Vienna to direct a movie. Nor had we corresponded regularly. During the night of October 2, I awoke, shivering, chills running down my back, my bed wet with sweat. I cried out: "Don't let him die, God, don't let him die!" I jumped out of bed, turned on the light, and paced the room. I felt drawn irresistibly to him in Vienna. It was an excruciating experience, as if I were splitting into parts. I tried to concentrate on my physical surroundings, on the possible, but it was useless. Finally, exhausted, I fell on my bed.

When I awoke, it was morning. I had no clear feeling, only a dull sensation that something was happening, as before a thunderstorm. I didn't know then what it was. What had happened during the night I dismissed as a bad dream. After all, I had not heard my father was ill, and such things just can't happen. So I went to the office and did my work. As usual I went to my boarding house for lunch. As I entered the hall I saw a telegram on the table. I walked slowly toward it. I knew it was for me. I knew what was in it. It was the wire saying that my father had died in the night. When I reached Vienna, I learned that he had had pneumonia and was recovering but could not resist the temptation to get up and do some work on an unfinished manuscript. A little clot of blood in his veins began to move toward his heart, and his heart stopped. He was only fifty-four years old. The little Mozart love song, *Eine kleine Nachtmusik*, was played at the funeral service.

In Vienna I became aware that the Nazi terror was increasing its efficiency. Coming from Copenhagen I had stopped overnight in Berlin at the home of an uncle. Before I left Austria, I got an urgent wire from my uncle warning me not to return through Germany; the Nazis had been to the house looking for me. I heeded the warning. I had known I was under surveillance in London; apparently it was to continue. And it did for the next seven years. I was trailed through Denmark and Sweden and finally across the Atlantic to Mexico. I always had the feeling I was being shadowed and so always carried a gun. Death was in the air. A friend of mine who was dating a beautiful German girl in Stockholm lost his life one night when she pushed him into one of the city's waterways. It happened she was a Gestapo agent.

The period from 1935 to 1938 was for me an interlude during which I made little direct progress toward my life goals. I did, though, study physics and other sciences in evening classes at the University of Stockholm and tried to apply natural science to the puzzle of good and evil. I didn't get very far. It was a blind alley. The Walt Disney job, however, turned out well, especially in Sweden. There, at a friend's home in Stockholm, on the second day of Christmas, 1935, I met Rita Emanuel, the girl who on August 30, 1936, became my wife. It really wasn't that cut-and-dried, for at the time I had not accumulated enough money to pay my debts, let alone support a family. This worried me, and one day I confessed my financial status to my fiance's father. "I don't believe under the circumstances I can afford the responsibility of marrying your daughter," I suggested. He responded quickly, "That's the first reasonable opinion I've heard from you. I'll call Rita in and we'll tell her." Rita came in and, having sized up the situation, proceeded to give both her father and me a dressing down such as I had never heard before. "What has a thing like money got to do with marriage?" she demanded. It was one of my best lessons in moral values, I think. The poor father, too, was bowled over, and agreed to sanction the marriage. Indeed, we were married in Riga, Latvia, which was where Rita's father happened to be engaged in organizing a textile factory, and he financed the wedding. Immediately afterward, Disney contracts began to come my way in Estonia, in Finland, and in Sweden, and we were on our feet.

I continued to keep a wary eye on the Nazis and to keep thinking of America as my ultimate destination. We organized our whole life on the premise that one day we might have to leave right away. We kept our money in a safe at home, rather than in a bank which Hitler might somehow take over.

For nearly four years we had an open ticket to New York on the Swedish-American line, so we could grab the next boat. We kept our American visas alive. And every three months we rehearsed packing for a quick getaway. After May 23, 1938, this included getting our son Jan ready for ocean travel. Finally, on the day of Munich, September 30, 1938, we packed for real; it was time for us to get as far from the Nazis as we could.

We went first to Hollywood to talk with Disney, and it ended with my going to Mexico City as the Disney man for Mexico and Central America. It was the middle of 1941, then, before I finally faced seriously the question of terminating my business career, emigrating to the United States, finding a teaching job again, and taking up in earnest my search for a way to organize good.

By this time my brother Henry, too, had left Germany and was living in New York City. I went to the U. S. Consul's office in Mexico City and applied for visitors' visas for my wife, Jan and me to go see my brother. At that time I was not a citizen of any country. The Nazis had expatriated me, and I was traveling on a Swedish alien's passport. While we were discussing our status with the consul, he suddenly opened a drawer and said: "I have just three immigration (not visitor) visas left. I offer them to you." As he was saying this, a second consular official came in. "Man," he said, "don't you know you may be ruining this man's life?" He turned to me. "What do you want in life?" he asked. "Oh, I guess I want to live happily," I answered. "Are you living happily?" "Yes." "Do you have a job?" "Yes." "Will you have a job if you go to the United States?" "No." "Do you have money?" "Yes." "Pesos?" "Yes." "Do you know how much they will be in dollars?" "Yes, it won't be too much." "Do you know we may be in the war?" "Yes." "Do you know you may be a soldier?" "Yes." "Do you know how it is to get a job in the States?" "No." "Well, it will be tough. See," he said, turning back to the first consul, "you're ruining this man's life." "Well," said the first consul, "I'll give you until tomorrow morning to decide," and he pushed the drawer shut.

My wife and I debated all night what to do, whether to stay in Mexico and live comfortably with plenty of money or to go to the United States and return to studying and teaching. The next morning I went back to the consul and said we'd take the immigration visas.

In New York I put my fate in the hands of a teachers' employment agency. Nothing turned up for awhile and I started to sell vacuum cleaners. "It beats as it sweeps as it cleans" was the slogan I quoted to New York housewives, and I managed to sell one cleaner: my commission, $8.35. Fortunately, before too long the agency did turn up a job for me teaching language, and later philosophy and history, at Lake Forest Academy in Illinois. This also enabled me to enroll at Northwestern University in Evanston in 1942 to work for my doctor's degree in philosophy. When I took out my first citizenship papers, I had said I would serve if drafted, but my only draft consisted of an assignment from the Office of Strategic Services to "lecture" Germans in the front lines over loud speakers, and the war ended before I could leave Lake Forest.

So at last I was all set to start teaching again the answers to the many questions on life, death, and human values which had never – even during the lucrative Disney years – ceased to plague me. I was about ready to pick up where I left off just before I went to Berlin's Charity Hospital.

Chapter Two

WHAT IS GOOD?

1. The Quest

One day, as a young fellow, I put down in my diary as the th   ..5
of my life: first, to find the true reasons for war; second, to teh   ..ie about
those reasons; third, to study law as the pattern of social and public life and
thus, I thought, the pattern of rationality.

By the time I began to teach at Lake Forest Academy and at the same time
to work for my doctorate in philosophy at Northwestern University, I had
sharpened my life's objectives somewhat. I had seen Hitler organize evil,
and I had determined to try to organize good. I had become convinced that
the organization of good involved finding out about war and how to stop it.
But I could see that to organize good I had to know "What is good?" This
is the question that began to put meaning into my life. If this question could
be answered, then perhaps good *could* be organized – scientifically – and
perhaps we could recognize human values as surely and sensitively as
material values. Then perhaps human dignity and worth could in time
triumph over human folly, peace could prevail, and civilization would be
free to advance. Indeed, I thought, this will have to be the case. Either we
know goodness, know value, and act accordingly, or we perish. There is no
other alternative.

I had also discovered that law would not help much in the search for what
is good. I had thought that judges always say who and what is right and who
and what is wrong, so they must know what is good and what is evil. But
when I got my law degree from the University of Berlin in 1932, I hadn't
learned a single thing from law about good and bad. The law doesn't say.
It tells only what is legal and illegal. It is an instrument that can be used for
good or evil. Law, like science, is morally neutral. With science you can
make the Sahara bloom or you can turn the world into a desert. With law you
can make evil look good by making it legal. Thus, it is legal, though immoral, to incinerate millions of people in war, and you might even get a
medal for doing it, but if you kill one person in peace, it isn't legal and you
may get the electric chair.

The Remer case in Germany is a good example of the moral neutrality
of the law. The case arose out of the unsuccessful bomb plot against Hitler's
life on July 20, 1944. The suitcase containing the bomb had been placed
under the table at which Hitler was to sit in his East Prussian headquarters
that day. The suitcase, however, got pushed away; and when the bomb
exploded, the Führer was not injured. Watching outside, Col. Schenk von
Stauffenberg, one of the conspirators, saw the explosion and mistakenly
assumed the bomb had hit its mark. He went to Berlin and told his fellow

conspirators that Hitler was dead. They immediately started taking over. Remer, in charge of the Berlin guard battalion, was ordered to arrest Joseph Goebbels, the propaganda minister. He marched his men into Goebbels' office and said, "Hitler's dead; I am here to arrest you." Goebbels said, "Man, you're mad. Hitler's alive." Remer said, "Prove it." Goebbels took the telephone, got the connection with Hitler, gave Remer the phone and Remer listened. "Mein Führer! Yes, sir!" He had recognized the voice immediately. Instead of arresting Goebbels he went back to arrest the people who had ordered him to arrest Goebbels.

After the war, Remer, during an election speech for his neo-Nazi party, called to a heckler, who was a son of one of the conspirators against Hitler's life, "You son of a traitor, shut up!" That young man sued Remer for slander. The German law court then had to decide whether Remer had slandered, or had spoken the truth. That meant to decide whether the men who tried to kill Hitler were traitors against Germany or were patriots; and this in turn meant to decide whether the government of Hitler was an honest-to-goodness government or some sort of murder gang, a non-government, so to speak. The case went all the way up to the Supreme Court, and the judges got opinions from priests and pastors and rabbis, from professors of philosophy and political science and from theologians. (All the opinions are gathered in a fascinating book, published in German, *The Remer Case*.) The judgment was: Remer had slandered the young man. The government of Hitler was no government, it was a gang which had usurped power. To get rid of Hitler was the duty of every German, and the father of that young man had tried to do his duty and therefore Remer had to go to prison for three months.

Now if Hitler had been in power again on the date of that Supreme Court decision, those very same judges, with the very same legality, would have said exactly the opposite. That is the law.

I'm not saying that law is no good, understand. We could not get along without it. It helped me a lot in making contracts and other legal arrangements when I was working for Walt Disney. It also helped me to think with more precision. But I knew that I would have to look elsewhere for clues to what is good. The law is morally neutral.

A. Frustration in Philosophy

So philosophy.

For four years I read and thought and contemplated philosophy and philosophers at Northwestern. With relation to my question, "What is good?", it seemed at the time to be a frustrating period. When I received my Ph.D. in 1946, I wasn't too sure but what my greatest achievement had been to learn what *wasn't* known.

Philosophers are aware that man has developed lopsidedly, that his knowledge of the world has dangerously outstripped his knowledge of himself, that he has learned to value and control nature but not how to value and control himself. They note with concern that even as he prepares for planetary travel, he continues to live in the Stone Age emotionally. Natural Science has changed the physical way we live so much that Julius Caesar or Columbus would not comprehend it. Unfortunately, it is equally certain that Jesus Christ would find mankind little changed. For the inner landscape in which he was interested and where he hoped to establish the Kingdom of God looks as barren and sterile, as chaotic and anarchic, as neglected and uncultivated as in his day. In this landscape the whole work of cultivation is still to be done – the clearing and plowing, the building of highways and lines of communication.

The trouble is that though they have tried hard, philosophers – like other students and scientists of life – have thus far failed to discover how to go about closing the great and ever-widening gap between physical nature and moral nature. Philosophers from Plato on down through the ages have tried to establish a moral science, a science of value, that would be to the social sciences – and so to the world of human relations – what mathematics is to the natural sciences. But these efforts may well be said to have been the most frustrating in the whole history of philosophy.

Plato proposed an institute whose members were to be asked to relate the laws which control the stars "to the institutions and rules of ethics." But nothing came of it. Descartes sought to formulate a "mathematical morality." Leibniz saw the differential calculus as part of a large calculus of universal logic applicable to all the sciences and humanities, so that "two philosophers who disagreed about a particular point instead of arguing fruitlessly would take out their pencils and calculate." Spinoza applied geometrical methods to ethics. As late as 1695, Locke believed natural science to be impossible, despite "the incomparable Mr. Newton," but he never doubted the possibility of a scientific *ethics* as obvious and precise as mathematics.

But all these philosophers failed to build the moral science they regarded as possible and necessary. They failed, in my opinion now, because they used the empirical methods of natural science; and ethics, or moral values, would not be harnessed by empirical methods – experiment, observation, and prediction. When they were applied, ethics turned into something like psychology or sociology and vanished. This ethics, I learned, is very elusive game and you have to approach her just right.

The autonomous character of ethics had been noted by Plato. It was observed in modern times by Immanuel Kant. Then in the present century it was pin-pointed by the English philosopher, George E. Moore. In his writing, which I studied assiduously at Northwestern, I began to find warm clues to what I was looking for, the answer to "What is good?"

When Plato in his day asked the question, he answered evasively that the interesting thing about goodness is the great difficulty to find what it is that all good things have in common. The Sophists and others talked about usefulness, pleasure, satisfaction, and purpose as being good; but, said Plato, these were kinds of goodness, not goodness itself. What he was after was the goodness that each of those things has in common. To use my own examples, what is it that a good microphone, a good cheese, a good person, a good automobile, and a good wife have in common?

There is a famous passage in Plato's *The Republic*. Glaucon says to Socrates, "Now, old man, you have talked about the problem aplenty -- tell us the solution." Socrates says,

> My dear Glaucon, the solution does not belong in this dialogue. For this we have to have another dialogue. I can't tell you what goodness is, I can only tell you what it is like. It is like the sun that radiates everything, that warms everything, that makes everything fertile and brings forth every-thing.

Glaucon implies that this is a poor answer.

We students of philosophy at Northwestern thought it was a poor answer, too, and we looked for that other dialogue where Plato gives the answer, but it was never written. It doesn't exist. So we went to Aristotle. Aristotle, in his *Ethics*, says there are many good things and they may or may not have something in common which is goodness; in any case, this is a problem that doesn't belong in this particular treatise. So we're stuck again. Believe it or not, you go through the whole of philosophy and nowhere do you find the solution to the problem of what is goodness in general.

B. The G. E. Moore Clue

Now we come, as I did in my work at Northwestern, to G. E. Moore. In 1903 Moore wrote a book called *Principia Ethica* adapting the title from Sir Isaac Newton's *Philosophiae Naturalis Principia Mathematica – Mathematical Principles of Natural Philosophy –* written in 1686. On the contents of this book is based our whole technological civilization, including the atomic bomb. It was Newton who enabled natural science to emerge from natural philosophy. Before Newton there was little natural science, just natural philosophy. Before Newton, these pseudo-sciences could not become chemistry and astronomy.

Moore wrote *Principia Ethica* as the introduction and foundation for a true science of ethics. He showed that throughout history philosophers, paying no heed to Plato, had continued to make a big mistake: they had mistaken kinds of goodness for goodness itself. They had confused genus and species. This confusion he called the naturalistic fallacy. Thus, negatively, Moore cleared away much ages-old philosophical garbage. Positively, however, he found the going rough. What is goodness itself? Well, he said, goodness only knows, I don't. Nobody knows. I know that goodness is but not what it is. His book, though fundamental, is short.

But Moore was unhappy that he didn't know and all his life he kept trying to figure out "what in the world" – as he so often expressed himself – goodness could be. Nearly 20 years after *Principia Ethica*, in 1922, he wrote a little essay entitled "The Conception of Intrinsic Value" in which he said "I still can't define good but now I can give an exact determination of it. Good," he said, "is not a sensory property; it has nothing to do with the senses. It is not a descriptive property, such as 'tall,' 'green,' or 'long,' or any property that you can see, hear, smell, touch, or taste. Good is none of those things, and yet," he said, *"good depends entirely on those sensory properties of the thing that is said to be good."*

Here is what Moore meant. Suppose Jim and John are to meet at Jim's car in the parking lot. "Which is your car?" John asks. "Oh, it's a good car," Jim says. Will John ever find the car? No, because "good" is not a descriptive property. Yet at the same time John has been told quite a bit about Jim's car. He knows it has an engine which runs, a gas pedal which accelerates, brakes which brake, tires, doors, seats, etc. If it didn't have those properties, it certainly would not be a good car.

For another example, take Swiss cheese. Swiss cheese has a certain smell, it has holes, it has a certain kind of density, it has a certain taste, and other sensory, descriptive properties. But, says Moore, goodness is not any one of these properties to which one's senses can respond. You can't see it, you can't smell it, you can't feel it, you can't taste it, you can't hear it. Yet, he said in 1922 in his *Philosophical Studies*, goodness depends entirely on that set of sensory, descriptive properties. But, he concluded lamely, I don't know how it depends.

Twenty years later, in 1942, George E. Moore was still in the dark, and he wrote, "If I knew in which way goodness depends on the descriptive properties, then I would know the nature of goodness, and I would have solved the old Platonic problem." But he died sixteen years later without having solved it.

So there we were, poor students in philosophy, especially me who wanted to find out what goodness is, left up in the air. Moore had been forced to conclude that goodness was indefinable, and that what the naturalists defined was not goodness but good things. So where was I to go from there? If Moore was wrong, then there was no goodness in itself; if he was right, then it was not definable. In either case it hardly seemed worthwhile to go on trying to solve the puzzle. But to admit that would be to admit that meaning had dropped out of my life.

Just about this time, the first atomic bombs were dropped on Japan. I knew I must continue my search for an answer, matter how frustrating. Now we knew how to make a bomb that would destroy hundreds of thousands of people, but we still didn't seem to know how to make ourselves good men. We might blow up our whole world before enough of us could find out.

C. The Search Renewed

There occurred to me one day in my dilemma this thought: perhaps Moore and his naturalist adversaries were partly right and partly wrong. Perhaps Moore was right in insisting on the uniqueness of good and the naturalists were right in insisting on the scientific approach to the quest for good; perhaps Moore was wrong in saying it was indefinable and the naturalists were wrong in committing the naturalistic fallacy, i.e., in confusing good things with goodness itself.

If so, how then was goodness in itself to be defined? I took a shot at the answer in my doctoral dissertation. I defined universal goodness as a feature of any situation. Every situation, I said, is a small part of the time process. Any process to be good must be one in which one situation follows another. The goodness of each situation, then, is that property in the situation which leads on to the next; it is the potentiality of the succeeding situation. And the next situation is good insofar as it fulfills the potentiality of the preceding situation. I elaborated this thought with the help of geometry and the concept of field theory in physics, and I titled my dissertation, *Can Field Theory Be Applied to Ethics?* I got my doctor's degree, but I felt vaguely dissatisfied, and as I taught philosophy the next few years in Ohio at the College of Wooster, corrected tests, and marked some of the papers "good" and others "fair" it struck me that what I was doing did not conform to my theory at all. Calling a paper "good" certainly did not determine the potentiality of a situation, except by some devious interpretation; and I did not mark it "good" because it fulfilled the potentiality of a situation. I marked it "good" because it was adequate to the subject. My dissertation had been all wrong. I had committed the naturalistic fallacy by confusing goodness itself with a thing that was good, namely, the potentiality of a situation.

The nature of goodness itself could only be approached, I decided, through analysis of the word "good."

I spent several years thinking about that word. Whenever I read or heard it, I noted its use. In the *Oxford English Dictionary* I found 135 uses and in Grimm's *Dictionary of the German Language*, 528 quarto columns. Eventually I had collected thousands of samples, by which time (1948) I had left Wooster to teach philosophy at the Ohio State University at Columbus.

Now what had all these uses in common? I spent most of my sabbatical time in 1949 trying to wring the answer from my piles and piles of evidence. Finally, on the afternoon of the day before Christmas, as I was putting a book back onto a shelf in my study, it suddenly hit me, out of the blue, and I knew I had it.

In my diary that Christmas eve I wrote: "Finally found the solution for the logic of good: 'x (anything) is a good member of its class means that x is a member of the class and has all the properties of the class.'" On Christmas day I wrote: "Another great day of creation. Extrinsic goodness defined. Intrinsic goodness defined." And to prove, I suppose, that I still had my feet on the ground, I concluded my entry: "Rita concocted a perfect duck."

D. The Moorean Puzzle Solved

My solution to the Moorean puzzle was as follows: Good has to do with *concepts*, not objects. When a person understands that a thing "is good" he doesn't need to know anything of the thing in question, but he must know something of the concept of which the thing is an instance. In the case of the car in the parking lot, for John to understand what Jim means about the goodness of his automobile, John doesn't need to know about Jim's automobile at all – therefore he will not be able to find it – but he must know something of the concept "automobile" of which Jim's car is a sample. He must know what an auto is, but he does not have to know what one specific auto is. Whenever we hear the word "good," we perform a logical operation: we combine the *properties of the thing* which we have in our minds with the idea of the thing in question. We give to the particular auto, for example, of which we may know nothing, the properties of automobiles in general, of which we must know something. From this logical operation is derived the *definition* of good, that is, of that which all good things have in common: *A thing is good when it has all the properties it is supposed to have, or put another way, a thing is good when it fulfills its definition.* In other words, goodness is the fulfillment of anything's concept or definition.

E. Is This Objective?

A good microphone is one that has all the properties a microphone is supposed to have. A good cheese is one that has all the properties a cheese is supposed to have. A good person is one who has all the properties a person is supposed to have. A good wife is one who has all the properties a wife is supposed to have. Or, in general, a good x is an x that has all the properties an x is supposed to have. I had found a universal definition of "good."

This means that we are defining good here in the general sense and not in the moral sense of right or wrong. When I say, "He is a good murderer," I do not mean that *morally*. I mean that he murders well. This does not mean, of course, that he is morally *good*. If I say, "She's a good girl," I don't mean it morally, I mean it in the sense that she has everything – all the properties – a girl should have; morally, she might be a bad girl. I mean, in other words, goodness in general, not moral goodness.

How do you know what properties a thing is supposed to have? You learn them as you grow up, from your parents, your teachers, your books, the dictionary, and your own common sense experience. When my little boy first came to the ocean, he looked in, saw a reflection and said, "Daddy, mirror!" I added another property to his definition of mirror. I said, "Such a *liquid* mirror is called water."

The week after that Christmas of 1949 I went to a philosophical association meeting at Worcester, Massachusetts. On the train I sat up all night thinking about my "creation," almost in a trance. It dawned on me that the embryo in my mind was not just ethics but a science which could be used as a frame of reference not only for ethics but for all the moral and social sciences. On New Year's Eve I wrote in my diary, "I feel good." And I thought, that's precisely the word with which to end the year.

What was coming out of me, then, was the science of formal axiology (from the Greek *axios*, valuable, worthy). Now "axiology" as value theory is nothing new to philosophy. It's defined in every dictionary and has been studied ever since Plato. But the notion of "formal axiology" is something else. The term was coined in 1903 by the German philosopher Edmund Husserl, who, like others, tried in vain to develop the concept systematically. It is the science which G. E. Moore in that same year foresaw and prepared for but failed to bring about.

Like mathematics, formal axiology is a kind of logic, though a different kind, and it is formal in that it has for its foundation a formal axiom (the definition of good) that results in a value system which is consistent, universally applicable, and historically continuous. It is applicable because the value axiom is based on the observation of value reality – the thousands of samples of the word "good" from which I distilled, so to speak, the axiom. The system that grows out of the axiom, then, can do for value sciences and value situations what mathematics does for natural (physical) sciences and natural situations.

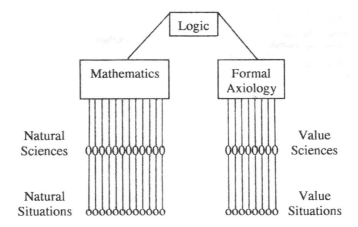

Science in general is neither natural nor moral science. It's simply *science*. It's *the application of a logical frame of reference to a set of objects.* In other words, science in general is a method, and it has nothing to do with the content, or subject matter, of any particular science. Today we have the natural sciences – physics, chemistry, astronomy, etc. – which are mathematically ordered. But the value or social sciences – politics, ethics, management, sociology, psychology, etc. – have had no framework corresponding to mathematics with which they could be ordered. Actually, they are philosophies, not sciences.

We have on the one hand Einsteinian physics and, on the other, Aristotelian ethics. Aristotle wrote a book about physics, too, but his physics is no longer taught because it's all wrong. Aristotelian ethics is just as wrong as Aristotelian physics, but it is still taught. I taught it myself for awhile with the other philosophical ethics, and my students would come to me afterward and say, "Do we know now how to be good men?" "Well," I'd hedge, "you're supposed to." "But," they said, "we don't." I couldn't help but agree, and my students were always disappointed and depressed. In the absence of an ordering logic and science of value, we find it difficult to realize the fruits of good will and good intentions because we don't know exactly what it is we want to realize.

The remedy, I believe, is to lift the social disciplines, the so-called humanities, to the level of sciences. Then we could know with exactness about goodness and value. Then moral, religious, political, sociological, and other phenomena which are vague, badly defined and hence badly understood, could become objects of an exact science. We could become more aware of the importance of the miracles and problems of everyday living, the things that really matter – the beauty of God's world, the laughter of children, the suffering of men, the importance of love and compassion.

By the close of 1949 I was sure that formal axiology could be the ordering logic for the value sciences. But my first writing efforts to tell my colleagues about my discoveries and their potentialities failed to stir much enthusiasm. They were politely interested but, as some told me, uncomprehending. Then came the annual meeting May 3, 1951, of the Western Division of the American Philosophical Association at Evanston, Illinois. I was to give a paper on "A Logical Definition of Value." Rita wrote to her mother:

> He was about to present his new logical theory for the concept 'good' on which he had been working uninterruptedly for two years. This is a completely new idea in philosophy, and it could go entirely wrong and he would be laughed at. No wonder both of us were very nervous. But the otherwise so quiet philosophers were electrified, and it was obvious that the last years were neither a waste of time nor a sacrifice. After the meeting the people stood around as if magnetized and could hardly wait to get rid of their questions. Everyone congratulated him, and they congratulated me, too.

Delivering my talk, I had sensed first that my audience was unbelieving; then, when they caught the gist, they became intrigued with the unfolding of my system; and I knew they were with me. The discussion was both lively and long. They wanted to go on and on and not go to the next paper. "The good makes people feel good," I wrote in my diary. "What seems to bring about this feeling is the contrast between the complexity of the problem and the simplicity of the solution."

In any event, formal axiology – value science – appeared to have come to stay. Appeared, I say, for though the audience of philosophers showed enthusiasm, it was an enthusiasm for the presentation; it was not based, I fear, upon an understanding of formal axiology. As Paul Weiss, Sterling Professor of Philosophy at Yale, puts it, the majority of philosophers in the U. S. ignore me, though some are kind enough to say that my work may well outlast my lifetime. I have had better luck in Latin America, where my work is studied, translated and discussed.

2. The Meaning

Fortified with the axiom of value science – a thing is good when it has all the properties it is supposed to have – I set out to expound it, to make it applicable to every day and every person; to, in other words, *make good measurable and organizable.* This work has claimed most of my attention for twelve years, during which I've taught formal axiology at Ohio State, the Massachusetts Institute of Technology, and (for six years now) at the National University of Mexico in Mexico City. In articles, pamphlets, books, and lectures I have expounded the science of value to colleagues in philosophy and the humanities throughout North and Latin America, to my students, and to management people in some of the largest corporations in the United States and Mexico. My work in developing the theory and practice of industrial profit-sharing – I was chairman of the organizing committee of the Council of Profit-Sharing Industries in the United States – is a result of applying axiology to economic theory. Similarly, I have tried to apply axiology to other social and humanistic disciplines such as political science, psychology, and ethics.

When one reflects that more human beings have been killed by other human beings in this century than in all previous recorded history, it is not hard to conclude that some things have gone wrong. The diagnosis is that of anomie, of lack of moral values. We cannot afford any more, as could earlier ages, to be bad; that is to invite annihilation. Peace and cooperation have now become pragmatic necessities for man's survival, and this calls for a reformation. Humanity, I believe, has never been in such dire need of a science which, by attuning us to moral values as sensitively as we are now attuned to technological and material values, can spark that revolution.

For the first time in history, I believe, such a system is possible. For the first time, I feel, scientific knowledge and mastery of physical nature can be matched by scientific knowledge and mastery of our moral nature. Natural science has changed the world; value science, too, once it is known, developed, and applied, is bound to change the world.

What follows, then, is an attempt to de-mystify and sensitize, to make the vague, the intuitive, and the chaotic in the world of human values intellectually clear, to show how formal axiology can lead to awareness of the several worlds we live in, to suggest a meaningful score for what could be a harmony of human life.

A. What is a good 'I'?

It's fairly simple to apply the axiom of value science to such things as apples, oranges, chairs, tables, microphones, and airlines. But what in the world is a good person? What makes *me* good? I am good, according to the axiom, if I have all the properties I'm supposed to have. Obviously, only I can define myself, nobody else can. When I first asked myself what I am, I said, "Well, I'm a philosophy professor." But that's not me; it's only part of me. And it's not what my wife married. When she married me she didn't even know I was a philosopher. I was a lawyer and businessman -- and perhaps not much of either. But she married me! Soon I saw that the question, "What am I?" wouldn't work. Philosopher? Yes. Husband? Yes. Father? Yes. Commuter? Yes. Eater? Yes. Speaker? Yes. Good Lord, I'm a million things. So when I tried to put down what I was in order to define what would be a good me, I had to draw this circle with a thousand segments.

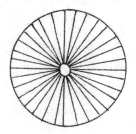

And I am together in the web of society with other such segments:

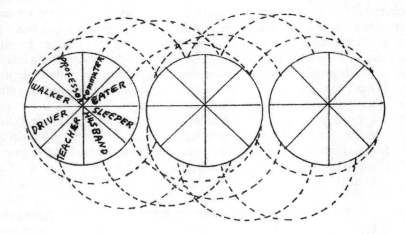

As a professor I'm among ten thousand other professors. I'm a husband among husbands, an eater among eaters, a sleeper among sleepers, a teacher among teachers. But where's me? Where's I? What is that which all these fragments of me have in common? Where's the core? So I had to ask, not what am I? but who am I? And I had to answer, I am I; I am the one that I am. This is the definition I have to fulfill. (In the *Bible* when Moses asked

God His name, God answered, "I am I" – I am the one I am, Yahweh. So it seems obvious; I am made in the image of God.)

The concept I have to fulfill, then, is 'I', and its meaning is "I am I." I must become conscious of myself, *Self*-conscious. But I must not confuse my *intrinsic, moral, inner* Self (with a capital *S*) with my *extrinsic, social, outer* self (with a small *s*). I must not confuse my fundamental 'I' with my social 'me,' the roles I play in society. To fulfill the definition of 'I,' ' I must be my Self.

The more I am aware of my Self, the more, and the more clearly, I define and fulfill my Self, the more I am a morally good person, a good 'I.' I am morally good if I am as I am. All the words of ethics mean this very same thing, this identification of myself with myself; being sincere, honest, genuine, true, having self-respect, integrity, authenticity.

To be your Self seems to be a simple thing, but it is most difficult to achieve. The catch is that it's not so easy for you to know who you are, and even more difficult, once you know, to fulfill this knowledge in your living. On the other hand, it is easy to kid yourself and not be your Self. I know. I was brought up strictly by my father and my teachers. In grade school we were beaten systematically and prophylactically in the German fashion. This was discipline. So I became a disciplinarian, a perfectionist, and I thought perfection was the highest value. My poor wife, though, didn't see life that way and thought there were higher values. I never knew what she suffered until I started to define my Self.

Most of us are not our Selves. We play roles. As an extreme example, I know a woman of 55 who pretends she is a girl of 18. She walks like 18, dresses like 18, and she's ridiculous – but she doesn't know it, for her Self is very poorly defined. Less obviously, many of us avoid fulfilling our Selves by just doing what we're told. We go along. But that's not us; that has nothing to do with the core of sincerity, honesty, and authenticity within us.

B. Three Parts of the Personality

Our inner or moral Self, our outer or social self, and our systemic or thinking self, comprise our total value pattern, our Personality. We can symbolize this value pattern as an inverted cone with a flag on top.

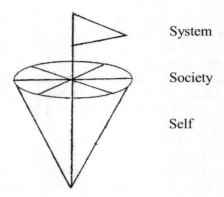

System

Society

Self

The levels or dimensions of our Personality may be known as the three S's – the Systemic, the Social, and the Self. The Systemic dimension relates to systems, laws, rules, regulations, procedures. The Social dimension relates to the segmented web called society; I think of it as our horizontal dimension, the part of us that, like the top of an iceberg, shows. The Self is our vertical dimension, our inner being, our conscience, our reservoir of infinite power which is there for us to use; in other words, our spiritual dimension. The cone of our being has infinite depth.

Systemic value is morally neutral, like the law, like science. We can't live without system, but we can overdo it. You have read about Adolf Eichmann. Was Eichmann a bad man? Not at all. He did his duty. He told the judges:

I never killed anybody. I was a transportation specialist. My work was to make railroad schedules. That's all I did. I followed my orders. It wasn't my business to know who was being put into those railroad cars, and where they went to. I just transported the people.

Well, he transported them to the fire, but that for him was incidental. He did it with great thoroughness and was proud of it. He was very systematic and the system was his life. In his cell in Jerusalem, he took every morning at the same hour so many steps in one direction, so many in another. He smoked exactly four cigarettes a day. Once, when he was interrupted and lost count, he was upset all day. Order, system: that was his supreme value.

You might say, well, that's a German for you. But it is not at all difficult to project this statement:

I'm the captain of a Polaris submarine. My submarine has sixteen nuclear bombs. Every one of these bombs has more firepower than all the bombs ever fired in all previous wars. If so ordered, I'll push the button and fire the bombs. That's my duty, to transport the fire to the people.

Once something was wrong with my railroad travel card. When I complained, the man called, "Miss Jones, bring me No. B33725." That was me – just a number. In the army you're a number, in prison you're a number, in the hospital you're a number. One nurse says to the other, "I'm giving a bath to 382." Number 382 is not even you – it's the room you're in. When your wife goes to the hospital to have her baby, she gets a number, the child also gets one, and you hope they'll match.

This is systemic value. It's necessary. It's important. It's like breathing. When you don't breathe, you suffocate. On the other hand you don't spend all your time thinking and talking about breathing, or doing nothing but breathing. In fact, doing too much breathing is just as unhealthy as doing too little. Too much emphasis on breathing may collide with and degrade other values. So with systemic value in general; it's not all-important, and sometimes it collides with and degrades more important values of the Personality. (A thing has value in the degree that it has properties. On the systemic level a thing has fewer properties than on the extrinsic and intrinsic levels, and it is less valuable.)

Now the *social dimension.* Here we get together with other people in a functional, recreational, or fellowship sense. Insurance people get together, professors get together, parents get together, school children get together. So the world is split up into many, many social or occupational groups, or classes. Everyone gets classified and is valued as an insurance agent, mechanic, teacher, housewife, mother, pupil, or what have you. This we call social value or extrinsic value. Money, for example, usually has only extrinsic value. But all social or extrinsic values are limited. You wouldn't sell your baby, or buy your wife, and there are many things that you know, deep down, are infinitely more valuable and more important to you than all the money and all the social prestige in the world. Extrinsically, a thing has more properties – and more value – than systemically, but its value still is bounded.

This brings us to the *Self dimension,* the 'I' in us. The 'I' dimension and its values need to be made as clear as possible, so clear that children can learn about them in day school and Sunday school. Here is where the person with meaning is separated from the person without meaning. Imagine chess pieces arrayed in a game between two masters. Suppose a gust of wind blows the pieces off the board. Nothing has been lost physically, but actually everything – all meaning – has been lost. That is the 'I' in relation to your total Personality.

Here in the inner Self is the real you, your 'I.' Here is where you can gain the concept of the person you are; here is the light that can reveal to you the whole world of Value, of the Good and the Evil that is within.

This 'I' level needs a close examination. For if we cannot define and become aware of ourselves, we are lost. If we can become aware of 'I' – develop the concept of our Self – and if we can *BE* that Self which we have defined, then we become a morally good 'I' and problems tend to fade away, for we come to know that human values are infinitely more important than social or material values, and hence than all efforts, political or technological, to change the world. As Larisa, in Boris Pasternak's *Dr. Zhivago*, says to her dear friend:

> The riddle of life, the riddle of death, the enchantment of genius, the enchantment of unadorned beauty – yes, yes, these things were ours. But the small worries of practical life – things like the reshaping of the planet – these things, no thank you, they are not for us.
> Little things like the reshaping of the planet!

Physical man may go to the moon, but he would still be in space and time. The inner Self is infinite. It leaps over and beyond space and time, it sees the whole of life at a glance. It remembers who I was yesterday and anticipates who I will be tomorrow.

It is the spiritual part of us which has made us, in the words of the psalmist, just a little lower than the angels. It makes life a thing of infinite value, infinite power, infinite compassion, and infinite moral goodness. It is our conscience which can lead us to the Kingdom of God within.

It has immediate intuition. It can pull body and mind and spirit together, give us integrity, sincerity, honesty, authenticity.

But it can, if undeveloped, if neglected, if denied, crack up into many fragments, and "we go all to pieces" or even become insane, coming closer to the realm of vegetables than to the sphere of angels.

C. The Inner Self Explained

Let me give you some examples of the inner Self at work. Some of you knew from the very first time you saw her that girl would be your wife. One of my girl students told me this:

> I was sitting in your class and in came a boy. I looked at him and I said to myself, there's my husband. Well, he sat with a friend at the other end of the room. After class, they went to a drug store and ate some ice cream. I sat down near them, and after three months we were married.

This is how I met my wife. When I was 25, I was at a friend's home in Stockholm admiring some fine dishes in a cabinet with a glass door. Suddenly I saw, among the dishes, the reflected face of a girl. She was standing behind me. And I said to myself, "There's my wife." Then I remember I said to myself, "You're crazy, man, you're 25. Men don't marry, only women do. Why give up your freedom at 25? Let the women do that." Then I said to myself "How do I know this is my wife?" And my answer was this: "Just as this is my little finger, this is my wife, and I can't do a thing about it." Rita told me much later that when I had gone, she turned to her mother and said, "I'm going to marry that guy." Her mother said, "You're crazy," and she was. For remember how I was raised, a disciplinarian, a perfectionist, a systemist. She had a rough row to hoe. But I found out through George E. Moore and through trying to define myself according to value logic that it was who, not what, that counts. As I became more aware of my *Self*, I found that our love was more important even than perfection. I became, I think, a different person and, says my wife, much better to live with.

This Self-awareness is different from knowing. Some people know everything but are aware of nothing, like the man in the Thurber cartoon about whom one woman whispered to another, "He doesn't know anything but facts." Others are aware of everything but know nothing. The first are informed fools, the second uninformed sages. The first are intellectuals without moral insight, the second are simple people with intuitive moral insight.

When we were in Mexico we had a maid named Maria. She came with us when she was sixteen and barefooted. At first she would sleep on the floor *beside* her bed. It took us a while to get her used to shoes and sheets. But she stayed with us for fifteen years, she ran the house, she ran us, she was aware of everything, but she knew hardly anything. She hardly knew that two plus two equals four. Yet there was a radiance and a spirit in her that made everything around her true and real. When she wasn't around, the world wasn't as it should be and we were depressed. When we lived at Lake Forest, she came to work for us there, and later went with us to Wooster and to Columbus, Ohio (when I was at OSU). When she was thirty-one, she married a fellow from Mexico, and they went to live in Chicago. We gave them introductions to six of our "egghead" friends there, suggesting that each let Maria work for them one day a week. Then we waited to see what would happen. It was hardly three weeks when the wife of one of our friends, a nationally known corporation lawyer, wrote to my wife, "What sort of a girl is this you have sent us? Whenever she comes to the house everything seems to be right. It's so peaceful and serene that my husband would much rather work at home on those days."

Knowing little, Maria has complete inner awareness and she *lives* completely. She is alive in her inner being, her Self dimension. All she has to do is *to be* – fully.

Now if you are not aware of your Self, you live only a little, and this is an ever-present danger in a socially well-organized society. It's so easy just to coast along. You may be a big shot, you may be wealthy, you may be the best man in your profession, you may be the most powerful man in the state, but if you don't have this Self-awareness, this inner life, you are nothing, you have not life. You have not fulfilled your Self. Though you may not know it, you have what Søren Kierkegaard, the great Danish philosopher, calls the "Sickness unto Death": to be alive to the world but dead to the spirit. Tolstoy tells about a man with this sickness in "The Death of Ivan Ilych." Ivan is a provincial judge with great ambitions to advance, so he pulls all the strings. He associates with the right people, and in due time he is named to the supreme court in Moscow. One day, while supervising the furnishing of his new home, he mounts a ladder to show the upholsterer how he wants the curtains hung, when suddenly he falls and injures his liver. It is a fatal injury, but liver injuries are lingering, and it takes him a long time to die. Meanwhile, his colleagues forget him; his friends fall away from him; even his family thinks he takes too long to die; and his only real friend is his peasant servant, who keeps his feet up and tries to make him comfortable. Tolstoy tells how Ivan Ilych comes to see how utterly trivial and meaningless his life has been. And before he dies, he has realized how through most of his life he has betrayed his reality and lived only on the surface. Reading the story you can follow almost page by page the process by which he slowly sloughed off layer after layer of his outer or social self and penetrated through his awareness to the core of his spiritual Self-awareness.

Maria by no means has this "sickness unto death." She is alive to the spirit, she is aware. She was alive to the world only in the cleaning of houses. But if you are alive to the spirit, your knowledge of the world will grow of itself, as you need it. As her husband made good at his job, Maria's world knowledge gradually widened, and they prospered. One evening about 9 o'clock when we were having guests at our home in Columbus, a long, expensive car stopped in front; and we wondered who that could be, for all our guests had arrived. Out climbed Maria, with her husband. They had come from Chicago to visit. Maria came in, gave us a bouquet of flowers, saw we were having a party, put on an apron and immediately took charge so my wife could be a hostess instead of spending time in the kitchen. Maria served, washed the dishes, cleaned the ash trays, and everything went fine. She explained they had just wanted to visit us, but before they left, she backed me into a corner and said, "Señor, I really came to tell you that we are pretty well off, and we're making a lot of money. You are just a professor, and I want you to know that whenever you are in trouble you are to call on us."

Maria, God bless her, is back in Mexico now, living in her own home and running her own business with her husband.

Now that kind of person is so fully *herself* that she doesn't have to give herself another thought. She just is. Her 'me' self (her social, functional self) is not in the way of her inner, moral Self, her 'I.' She is, as we call it, *transparent to herself*. She is free to pour all her energies into living for others. Such a person we call a saint. Maria is a small-gauge saint. A great saint would be a person who matches the depth of his own being with the width of his intellectual horizon. This was Jesus. This perhaps is Albert Schweitzer. And there are many other people – some of whom you undoubtedly know – who have saintly qualities in lesser and higher degrees.

Sometimes, unfortunately, our intellect blocks our attempt to become alive to the spirit within u – to become Self-aware. For to do so, you must be humble. Smartness doesn't help. You have to be, just be; you have to be natural and not pretend, not be proud or ashamed of this or that. You have to be able to put your worldly matters in their places. To be is probably the most difficult and, at the same time, the most important task of our moral lives. In daily life, it is highest maturity, and it is also very powerful for it brings into play the infinity of your intrinsic Self. To scramble around on the treadmill of extrinsic value is not only immature, it is inefficient, for it shuts up your infinite powers and lets them lie idle. It prevents you from really living.

Sometimes we approximate just being when we "get away from it all" on vacations, for then we are alone with ourselves and get acquainted with ourselves. The problem is to inject the vacation spirit into our daily lives.

So when students ask me what exactly it is just to be, I say, "It's very hard to explain. You must just be – don't be cocky, don't let your smartness get in the way of your being." "Well," one of my students may say, "if I'm not smart you give me bad grades." "Ah," I say, "I'm your teacher in philosophy, I'm not your teacher in Being. If I were your teacher in Being, you would get no grades at all, for everything in Being is infinite."

Some do understand, but most still do not. So I finally say, "Look here, your inner Self, your humble Being, is what makes dogs lick you. That's all." What I mean is that with
our inner Self we go down, down, down to the roots of creation. We have oneness with all living things. So the dogs think you are a dog – or they are people – and they come and lick you. Another sign of this Being is the reaction of children. My wife hardly gets into a room with children before they are all over her. (With me children are more reserved, but dogs go all out to lick me.) In school you've all known some teachers for whom the

whole class was noisy and others for whom the class was so quiet you could hear a pin drop. Children sense Personality; they respect a person who respects himself.

D. Infinity of the Inner Self

I've said that the inner Self – the 'I' that I am – is infinite, has infinite value, and is capable of boundless spiritual power and compassion. How do I know and what do I mean?

Well, Jesus demonstrated the infinite intrinsic value of a human being, though, as we shall see later, he used a metaphorical language to explain it, much different from the one we are now using. After Jesus, a young Italian, Pico della Mirandola, discovered, shortly before Columbus discovered America, the new world of man's infinite spirit. Pico wrote an "Oration on the Dignity of Man" in which he told this wonderful parable:

> The Best of Artisans... took man as a creature of indeterminate nature and, assigning him a place in the middle of the world, addressed him thus: 'Neither a fixed abode nor a form that is thine alone nor any function peculiar to thyself have We given thee, Adam, to the end that according to thy longing and according to thy judgment thou mayest have and possess whatever abode, whatever form, and whatever functions thou thyself shalt desire. The nature of all other beings is limited and constrained within the bounds of laws prescribed by Us. Thou, constrained by no limits, in accordance with thine own free will, in whose hand We have placed thee, shalt ordain for thyself the limits of thy nature. We have set thee at the world's center that thou mayest from thence more easily observe whatever is in the world. We have made thee neither of heaven nor of earth, neither mortal nor immortal, so that with freedom of choice and with honor, as though the maker and molder of thyself, thou mayest fashion thyself in whatever shape thou shalt prefer. Thou shalt have the power to degenerate into the lower forms of life, which are brutish. Thou shalt have the power, out of thy soul's judgment, to be reborn into the higher forms, which are divine.'[4]

In other words, says Pico, ours is the whole range of creation. We can just vegetate or we can rise on the wings of the spirit almost to God. We are not limited. We have infinite power. But it's up to us to make use of it.

When one of my students asks what a genius is, I tell him, "*You* could be a genius. For a genius is a person who applies infinite power to one problem." And when the student says, "But I don't have that kind of power," I say to his neighbor, "Try and strangle that guy. You'll see what power he develops."

There was in the newspapers the story of a little woman, weighing 110 pounds, whose son was lying in the garage under a two and a half ton car when the jack broke. The woman went into the garage, lifted that car from her boy, put her leg underneath and pulled him out, though she broke her own back in the process. Well, that's what we call a miracle, for a miracle is summoning and making use of the infinite resources within us.

After the war I talked with persons who had been "skeletons" weighing 50 to 60 pounds in the concentration camps in Germany. They told me how they had walked miles upon miles before they were freed as the Nazis chased them out of the concentration camps ahead of the advancing Americans. One survivor said: "We heard the American planes over us and whenever we heard them we got more power and we could walk and walk. I don't know where the power came from but we had it when we needed it."

You get your power in crises. A genius is in a continual crisis. He gets his power all the time. When you read the stories of men of science, like Newton, or of art like Bach or Michelangelo, you find that when asked their secret they gave almost the same answer: Anybody can do it who doesn't do anything else day and night. "I keep the problem continuously before my eyes," said Newton. "I *became* a falling body," said Galileo. "I live my poems," said Goethe. A genius puts his whole Self into a problem. He's not necessarily a good person morally – he's just a genius. There's a difference between a great man and a great *good* man. A great good man is a Saint, who puts his whole power, all his resources, into his own goodness. He has discovered his oneness with all creation – all men, all animals, even all things. He lives deeply and compassionately within every human being, indeed every living being. Albert Schweitzer feels pain at having to kill the bacteria when he does an operation. St. Francis said to Brother Leo when he tried to extinguish the fire burning St. Francis's coat tail: "Brother Leo, be careful with Brother Fire." Compassion is the touchstone of moral value.

Many of you, too, must feel pain and suffering when you see someone or something else unhappy and suffering. If you have this sensitivity, you know it comes from your awareness of oneness with all humanity, for your inner or intrinsic self is infinite in its reach and perception. In infinity all lines meet at the vertex of the infinite cone; that is, the 'I' meets all the vertices of all the other Selves. There's only *one* vertex of all the cones. At bottom they are all one.

That's why you can immediately know that girl is to be your wife. You are one with her, not in space and time but in the infinite depth of your own awareness. Love and friendship are not in space and time. I think most of us have had personal experiences that confirm this. After my wife, Baby Jan, and I left Sweden in 1938 to go to California, I went back to Sweden to close up my Disney business. One day, reading the paper in the home of my wife's parents in Stockholm, it flashed through my mind that my wife was ill. I felt it so vividly that I telephoned to California, and a nurse answered. She said, "Yes, your wife has been in a crisis, but it looks as though she will pull through all right." I expect many people could tell of similar experiences.

The infinity of the inner Self is vividly reflected in our *conscience* – con-science, a knowing together. You must be a co-knower of your Self to be your Self; i.e., you must identify your extrinsic self with your intrinsic Self, and at the same time identify your Self with everyone. Conscience, too, makes you one with everybody. When you have done something wrong, even though nobody was there and nobody saw you, afterward you feel guilty and as if everybody knows what you've done. Even the little bad things you do now and then give you what is called a "bad" conscience, meaning that you are afraid everyone knows with you. The classic story about this feeling-that-everybody-knows is Dostoevski's *Crime and Punishment*. A student kills an evil old woman for money. It's the perfect crime, yet he feels that everybody knows, for 700 pages. He finally gives himself up; he cannot live with his terrible guilt.

Now why do we have this feeling that everybody knows? Because we are one with everybody. The inner Self is not in space and time. It cannot be measured, it is eternal. Where is it? Everywhere. When is it? Always. In other words, since our inner Self has no limits, we are intrinsically one with every other Self. The cores of our Selfhood, as I said, all meet at the vertex. There is one community, one core, of all mankind. This is what Jesus calls the Kingdom of God within us. We are all one, and when we do a wrong thing everyone has done it with us. That is why we are afraid that everyone knows. I am responsible for everybody else and everybody else is responsible for me. This is the meaning of love. In the depth of the Self is the true reality; here we hurt and we help those we love -- and those we love ought to be all our fellow men. As the preacher in John Steinbeck's *Grapes of Wrath* says: "Maybe it's all men and all women we love; maybe that's the Holy Spirit – the human spirit – the whole shebang. Maybe all men got one big soul everybody's a part of."

In value science, conscience as an expression of intrinsic value precedes society as an expression of extrinsic value, and science, law, and other systems as expressions of systemic value. The particular precedence of intrinsic over systemic value is guaranteed the protection of the state in democratic nations, as in the First Amendment to the U. S. Constitution, in laws concerning conscientious objectors, and in similar statutes. Whenever the claims of conscience and science conflict, as happens when scientists balk at developing more deadly nuclear weapons, conscience must be free to follow its own course.

E. Logical Proofs of Self Infinity

It should be fairly obvious by now that personal experience attests to the infinite character of the inner or intrinsic Self. Human infinity is also a mathematical certainty which can be proved axiologically. It can also be proved logically. Two such proofs are known in philosophy as the Identity of the Self and the Infinite Regress of the 'I.' First the Identity proof.

What is the 'I'? It is that which makes one person out of the infinite fractions of your life in time and space. Every minute of your life you are different. You were a baby, you were in high school, you make a living, you will be old. Now you are sitting and reading, next you are eating, next you are visiting, next working. To be the same person, all these times and all these moments must be pulled together. All these moments must belong to *you*, the self-same person. You must be able to say: I was born 50 years ago, and I am now here. Thus, the 'I' pulls together our moments in space and time. It is the concept which makes out of your space-time moments one whole.

"I"

0 0 0 0 0 0 0 0 0 0 0 0 0 0 0 0 0 0 0 0 0 0 0 0 0 0 0

Me at Birth   Me Now   Me at Death

In other words all your me's pulled together are your 'I.' 'I' is the concept of the me's, the concept of your moments in time and space, your concept of identity. How many moments do you have in time? Fifty-two years, we'll say. How many days? 52 times 365, or 18,980 days. How many hours? 455,520. How many minutes? How many seconds? There is an infinity of subdivisions we can make. So you have an infinity of life moments, and all of them have to be pulled together.

But as a matter of fact, you didn't begin with your birth. You started with your conception. Once you go that far back, you find you didn't start there either. You started with your father and mother, and they had to be conceived, too, so you didn't start there either but with your grandparents and so on back and back. Actually you began with the beginning of creation. That's what Walt Whitman says in the "Song of Myself."

Immense have been the preparations for me...
For room to me stars kept aside in their own rings...
Before I was born out of my mother generations guided me,
My embryo has never been torpid, nothing could overlay it.
For it the nebula cohered to an orb,
The long slow strata plied to rest it on,
Vast vegetables gave it sustenance,
Monstrous sauroids transported it in their mouths and deposited it with care.
All forces have been steadily employed to complete and delight me,
Now on this spot I stand with my robust soul.

I'm a result of creation, of evolution. I began in infinity, and where do I end? Do I end with my death? Well, there's my son and my granddaughter. I am a link in the chain of generations on earth. Even though I have no children, my Self, my spirit, as I said, is not in space and time. How then can it die in space and time? It cannot die. Body and mind may fall away, but the spirit must go on to eternity. It is a peculiar thing that the inner Personality is in the genes, and the genes never die; they go on from generation to generation. Scientists have speculated as to why some persons have unusual affinities for certain kinds of life. At Yale University, for example, there is a famous spider specialist. He loves spiders and they love him. They crawl all over him, and he thinks they are the most interesting phenomena in the world. There are also snake specialists. When I was at Wooster, a friend of mine was an expert on the parasites of fish parasites, and he took a great liking to them. Now how does one happen to have such an affinity? Could it not be that the genes go back to the beginning of creation and repeat the whole of evolution in our embryonic development?

Even communists must acknowledge the infinite causal chain from which they have come. Even they must acknowledge that the 'I' pulls 'me' together, integrates 'me.' They, too, must agree that when the Self is sick or incapable of pulling the 'me's together, something very wrong is likely to happen. For they have their schizophrenics, their split personalities, just as we do. At the University of Mexico I have a seminar of psychoanalysts who are studying human values. We analyze some of their cases using the axiological method. One such case involves a housewife who is married to a rich businessman and has a lovely family and nice home in a suburb of the capital. She has the reputation of being a good housewife and a good mother. But every Tuesday and Thursday she goes, as she says, to play canasta with some girl friends. Actually, she goes to the slums of the city as a prostitute. She comes home at four in the morning and says she won money at canasta. Home, she cannot remember what has happened. She feels vaguely that something is wrong, so she goes to a psychoanalyst, and the story finally comes out. She has, you see, a multiple personality; she's two. She has a Self-contradiction within her. Her self-definition is not "I am I" but "I am not I." Fulfilling this definition, she splits apart. She can't live, she doesn't want to live. In order not to kill herself physically, however, she prostitutes herself and so kills herself morally. The money gives her a special satisfaction, a token of appreciation which she has never had before. Her husband has no idea of the situation, nor have the children, nor has she in a way because she doesn't know when she is one person what other person she is. She has a split identity.

You may remember the movie or the book, *Three Faces of Eve*, which told of a similar situation. And one of the most famous cases of split identity is, of course, that of Robert Louis Stevenson's Dr. Jekyll and Mr. Hyde.

In other words, when our 'I' does not pull us together, then we are not one but several, split up in our space and time sections – our 'me's – without connection, even though we are one body.

Normally, however, we come as one person from infinity; and we go to infinity. The German poet Goethe said, "I am immortal in the degree that I have lived immortally" – in the degree, that is, that I have lived in the fullness of my own awareness. I am, says Kierkegaard, anchored with my own Self at the source of creation. I not only express the infinitely many moments of my life on earth, I express the span of all life between the infinity that was and the infinity that is to be. I am a child of creation – Whitman was right – and I embrace creation. If I live like a vegetable, I have let down creation.

The 'I' Self then – not the 'me' self, not my body, not my mind – pulls the many time-space fragments of 'me' together, in the *awareness of itself*, and the knowledge of me. To achieve this integration, it must itself be outside space and time; it must use memory, anticipation, and imagination, but itself be none of these. Hence, though it uses my body, my corporeal presence, it must itself be beyond it, in infinity.

This is the first logical proof of the infinity of the Self. It is based on the logical principle that what involves a whole cannot itself be a part of that whole.

The second logical proof concerns the Infinite Regress of the 'I.'

When I say I know myself – or me, the extrinsic part of my being – the 'I' knows me, but who knows the 'I'? The 'I' who does the knowing knows only the 'me,' it doesn't know itself. There are two roles, that of a knower and that which is known. The knower is the 'I' and the known is the 'me.' The 'I' knows the 'me' by applying itself to the 'me' – my situations in space and time, my emotions, my thoughts, my goings, comings, and doings. *But just as the eye can see but cannot see itself, so the Self – the 'I' – can know, but cannot know itself.* To know 'I,' I have to make it a 'me.' I have to say: "I know me knowing me." Now I know the first 'I' as a 'me'; but there appears another 'I' that does the knowing and cannot be known. I can make a 'me' out of it and say, "I know me knowing me knowing me," and thus know the second 'I' as a 'me,' an object of knowledge; but there appears a third 'I' as subject of knowledge, and it cannot be known. And so on *ad infinitum*. There is always another 'I' or self that cannot be known. Thus, there are infinite levels within the Self. There is always a residue unknown to the 'I' which has to be known by something other than Self-knowledge. I can only be aware that there is this residue of myself.

Maria is a good example of the kind of person with this awareness. A widely circulated magazine has run a series of articles on the most "unforgettable characters I have known" and usually they are not big shots, but just simple people of great insight, sensitivity, compassion and dignity – Marias of one sort or another who live in awareness of others, who are Self-aware, and who are truly themselves without knowing it. They are like people who enjoy the symphony without knowing the score. Should they learn the score, they would enjoy the music even more.

F. The Opportunity to Live

Now let's backtrack a bit. You remember that a thing is good – has value – to the degree that it fulfills its definition. I have moral value to the degree that I fulfill my definition of my Self. To the degree that I am I, I am a morally good person. *Moral goodness is the depth of man's being himself*, and that is the greatest goodness in the world. For what we find within us when we penetrate to the roots of our Selves, no matter what route we take, can only be described as God. That is why, if everyone of us would be truly himself and follow the lead of his own inner Self, or as we say, the still, small voice of our conscience, then everything would begin to straighten itself out, and problems would fall by the wayside. We would know the true eternal values.

It is my conviction that through formal axiology the deep, eternal values of life can be made intellectually articulate. The trouble has been that these values have been known vaguely, intuitively in a shallow sense of the word, and that we haven't been able to articulate them. We always say that the difference between us and the Russians is that we believe in the value of the individual, that man is made in the image of God, that man is of infinite value. But they say these are just words, and challenge us to say what we mean. Many times we don't know. Many times our behavior says that we don't know.

I once met a newspaper publisher who said he was doing everything he could to propagate American values, the value of the individual. When I asked what he meant by the value of the individual, it turned out that he meant the individual's right to make a lot of money. So it is with many of us Americans. We play into the hands of the communists by putting money and other extrinsic values ahead of human value. The increase in juvenile delinquency, crime, corruption, and graft in American life is evidence of the leaks in our moral dikes. Violence is fast becoming part of the American way. Indeed, according to sociologist Lewis Yablonsky, a new kind of criminal is emerging, one who maims or kills and destroys for kicks and who has no regard for the rights and feelings of others.

These are the rotten fruits of moral frustration, the kind that Hitler and others like him have tasted. If mankind is to continue, we must help the search for moral fulfillment to succeed. We must articulate and differentiate the different levels or worlds of value so that we can knowingly choose our own being between vegetables and angels. We must let it be known that we have the opportunity to live in three worlds, the systemic world of rules, the social world of the senses, and the moral or spiritual world of our inner Selves – and therein to live balanced, meaningful lives.

Some people, unfortunately, live mostly in one world, some mostly in another. Some, for example, live almost completely in the systemic world of rules, laws, technology, and red tape. In their worship of the systemic beauty of this world, they ignore reality and human values. They appear in a spectrum of types from quiet, absent-minded professors to small- and broad-gauge Eichmans.

Ninety-five percent of the people in the developed countries, East and West, capitalist and communist, live mostly in the world of extrinsic value. The vast majority of them believe this is the only really important world there is, neglecting their inner Self, as did Tolstoy's Ivan Ilych. In the so-called underdeveloped countries, however, a great mass of humanity lives but little in the world of extrinsic value, of social classes and functions. They may live in the primitive world of strict ritual, of systemic values, but they also live in the world of their inner Selves, and the encroaching extrinsic world throws them into turmoil. "We May Be Rich But They Are Happy" was the title of an article by the British economist Barbara Ward in *The New York Times Magazine* (May 5, 1963) in which she pondered the question, "Will the spread of Western technology cause the people of Asia and Africa to lose their secret of self-fulfillment?" "Our technical society," she writes, "so wrapped up in means and manipulation, too often fails to give us direction and dedication, without which we can be rich and healthy and strong, yet bored and joyless as well."

Precisely. These people are underdeveloped only extrinsically. On the level of intrinsic value we are at least as underdeveloped as they, and often more so. We probably need rather urgently to *import* a *spiritual* program of foreign aid.

Each of us lives to some extent in the world of our inner Self. None of us lives there as deeply as we might. In fact, not even in the world of the systemic do we live as fully as we ought to and could. You and I know practically nothing of physics, of relativity, or quantum theory. Of a great part of the world we are ignorant. We are experts only at social living – and that is only one world among three. Thus we really live very limited lives. The complete human being would be he who knows all of science, has all the social experiences, and lives in the fullness of his inner Self. This perfect human being doesn't now exist, for we are still at a low stage of evolution. Compared to man in a billion years – if there is man in a billion years – we are like monkeys. I believe man in a billion years may be that full human being.

Most of us live so fully in the social world that we don't know the spiritual resources we have – until we are tested, perhaps, in crises in our lives. We are social animals with social intelligence. What we call a moron is actually someone who doesn't know how to get along in society, but he is a moron only in this extrinsic sense. In other respects he might be more intelligent than you or I. We may be scientific and spiritual morons as truly as he is a social moron.

Really, we live shallow lives. We live a small fragment of ourselves. Kierkegaard has said we live only in the basements of our houses. We are not fulfilling ourselves.

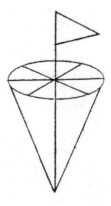

Of the full potential spectrum of man, we look maybe more like this –

like saucers rather than infinite cones, like tops rather than universes. And as children whip their tops around, so circumstances whip us around – till our heads spin. Only if we summon the resources within us do we begin to fulfill ourselves. That is the task that the present and the future have for man, and that each of us has for himself.

G. Three Worlds of Value

We live in three worlds; we also value in these three dimensions. We can value the world itself systemically, extrinsically, and intrinsically. Valued systemically, everything in it is consistent with everything else, everything must happen the way it does, and evil is merely a delusion. The world is perfect. This was Spinoza's view.

Valued extrinsically, the world is the totality of all natural and functional properties. Other worlds are thinkable, but if they are not the totality of all natural properties they lack some properties and thus, by our axiological definition, would not be as good as the world which is the totality of all properties. Since the world is the world of empirical things, extrinsic valuation is its proper valuation. This was the philosophical view of Leibniz.

Thirdly, the world can be valued intrinsically. In this case it is valued in the totality of its being-the-way-it-is and with the complete involvement of the valuer. This would be the view of a nature mystic such as Goethe.

Not only the entire world but anything in and out of it can be valued in each of these dimensions, whether a button, God, my wife or myself.

A button would be valued systemically as a product in a button factory, extrinsically as a useful part of a shirt, and intrinsically as an object to which a fetishist is devoted.

God is valued systemically in theology, extrinsically in comparative religion, and intrinsically by a person who makes God his problem or his way to personal salvation. God is the supreme value, the value of values. Nothing more valuable is thinkable.

My wife is valued systemically in her function as housekeeper or cook (a kind of animate household appliance), extrinsically in comparison with other women, and intrinsically in her own uniqueness and my love.

My self is valued systemically to the degree that I conform with my preconceived – and false – notion of my self (small s) as a system, extrinsically in comparison with others performing functions and playing roles in society, intrinsically in awareness of my Self (capital S) as a unique person – my being my Self naturally, genuinely, truly, sincerely, and honestly.

Every situation, it follows, has its systemic, extrinsic, and intrinsic value aspects, the choosing of a wife or husband, the choosing of the president or a file clerk of a company, or, for illustration, the flight of the Enola Gay to Hiroshima. The pilot wrote in the log book the wind velocity, the weather and everything; at this exact minute the bomb was released, angle so-and-so, weight so-and-so, weather so-and-so, etc. – all the mechanical, aerodynamic, meteorological details of the flight. But at the end of these entries in the log book are these words: "My God, what have we done?" Everything in the log book up to those last words is natural science – mathematics, physics, astronomy, chemistry – but those last words, "My God, what have we done?", are a moral valuation, in the field of intrinsic value. The pilot of the lead plane on the Hiroshima run, by the way, acquired such a guilt complex that later he could not hold a position in society and had to have psychiatric care.

Here is another example of valuation in three dimensions, some aspects of which probably every one of us has experienced. You are, let's say, a young fellow who goes into a store to buy cigarettes. You tell the girl at the counter, "I want a package of Soandso's." She says, "Here you are." "How much?" "Twenty-seven cents." You pay her, she thanks you. What kind of relationship was that? Purely systemic, a legal sales contract. The girl might as well have been a machine.

Next day you go into that same store and there is that same girl and you look at her and think, "My gosh, she's a girl," and you look again and think, "She looks pretty nice." You say, "How long have you been in town?" "Oh," she says, "three months." Soon you're talking with each other about the weather, the newspapers, your home towns, and so on. There is a social relationship. You have moved from the systemic, with its limited properties, to the extrinsic level, with its infinite properties. You could talk to her on and on; you like her.

Sooner or later you take her out to dinner and you have a wonderful time. Now you have added to your relationship. It has become richer, hence it has more value. There follow other evenings, and all the time your relationship with each other grows until it takes in your whole being. One day you say to her – or she says to you – "When do we marry?" And before you know it you stand in front of the minister with her and take your vows to love, honor and cherish her, for richer or poorer, for better or worse, in sickness and in health, until death do you part.

Now you've come a long way from the systemic cigarette contract. You are husband and wife, and a true love marriage has nothing whatever to do with a social relationship. It's a relationship from inner core to inner core, like this:

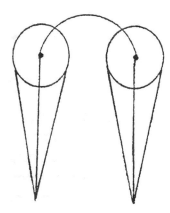

And she doesn't give a hang how much money you have or who your father and mother are, and you don't give a hang about her background, her money, her career. You love her, she loves you, and you get together. How do you know you love each other? Because I'm speaking of a real love marriage each of you has gone within your Self and has become aware of the other's Self. You have asked and found out "Who is this person?" And you see that young girl of 18 as the grandmother of your own grandchildren, when your own children haven't even been conceived. It's your inner Self, again, overleaping space and time.

H. Measurement of Value

To qualify as a true science of value, the laws of formal axiology must be universal, absolute, and valid for any rational being whatsoever, whether man, woman, or child, whether European, American, or Asian, whether on this planet or some other.

At present such universal laws are used in natural science and in music. Both physical science and music are applied mathematics. Mathematics, thus, is a more universal structure than either physical science or music. But mathematics is not yet the highest and absolute system; this is the system of rational thought itself, logic. Just as physical science and music are applied mathematics, so mathematics is applied logic. Thus, rational beings can communicate by the system of logic itself.

It happens that formal axiology, too, is applied logic, so it is possible for the theory of value, of goodness and morality, to be understood by rational beings everywhere.

The difference between natural science and value science is that the former applies to events, while the latter applies to the meanings of events. Value, we may say, is *meaning*. When we say that life has meaning we mean it has value. The richer its meaning, the richer its value. When we say that life has no meaning, we mean it has no value. The poorer its meaning, the poorer its value. A meaningless life is without value, is no good.

Formal axiology uses meaning as the measure of value, the standard which is valid for all kinds of value. The procedure is relatively simple, for meaning, logically, happens to have the form of a measure; it is a measure of value just as a yard is a measure of length or a pound a measure of weight.

Take a chair. The properties of a chair – four legs, a back, a seat about knee high, etc. – constitute a "set" and may be numbered, "1, 2, 3...." Each property is a unit of the set. A good chair, as we know by our axiom of value, is one which has all its properties, that is, has its full meaning as a chair. If the chair lacks a knee-high seat, or a back, or both, it is fair, poor, or bad. The words "good," "fair," "poor," "bad" are terms for measuring value, i.e., meaning, and are logically no different from the words "yard," "pound," "hour," "dozen," "degree," that measure length, weight, time, amount, and intensity respectively.

Thus, value theory is fundamentally as strictly logical as logic itself or mathematics or physics. Actually, meaning as the standard of value is more universal than physical measures or than number itself. Martians might not understand our number system – based on our ten fingers, "digits" – but they, too, will be calling *good* anything that fulfills its meaning and *bad* anything that does not.

Though the measure of value is universal and objective, it should be noted that *the application is subjective*. It may well be that what I call good you call bad, and vice versa. But this is a matter of application, not of axiology itself. If you are walking down the street with a friend and you see two people approaching and your friend, a little drunk, sees four, he is not invalidating mathematics, he is only using it wrongly. He is actually confirming mathematics just as you do. Neither of you made a mathematical mistake. His mistake was in seeing, not in adding. In the same way, whenever anybody thinks that a thing fulfills its meaning he will call it good, and whenever he thinks it does not he will call it bad, and thus he will confirm axiology. Whether he rightly or wrongly thinks that a thing fulfills its meaning is a different question – of application, not of axiology.

To measure value, then, you determine the degree to which a thing, a situation, or an individual fulfills its concept or meaning, the extent to which it has all its properties.

There are three kinds of concepts – synthetic, analytic, and singular (each of which will be explained).

Systemic value fulfills the synthetic concept.

Extrinsic value fulfills the analytic concept.

Intrinsic value fulfills the singular concept.

I. Systemic Value

Synthetic concepts are constructions of the mind, like geometrical circles. A geometrical circle is defined with such precision, "a plane closed curve equidistant from a center," that if a curve does not have all these properties and lacks just one of them, it isn't a bad circle, it's simply not a circle. For the same reason there are no bad electrons. When a thing seems like an electron but lacks an electron property, we can't call it an electron, and a main endeavor of modern physics is to find out about these "bad" electrons and give them new names – positron, meson, etc. There are no bad square roots of minus one for the same reason. Why is there equity in the law? Because even in the law there are such exact definitions that when a thing lacks a part of the definition it is not what it is defined to be; yet, justice must be done even if the case does not exactly fit.

A synthetic concept has a definite or finite number of properties, then, which may be symbolized as n. It gives rise to only two values, either perfection or non-existence, value or non-value. There are no degrees of value, such as good, fair, poor, and bad. Everything is either black or white.

A systemic state or organization (the fulfillment of a synthetic concept) is authoritarian, dictatorial. You either belong, or you get out. Shades and differences of opinion and character are not tolerated. Individuality is cancelled. The one value is conformity, and the one disvalue, non-conformity, which leads to expulsion or "liquidation."

The world of systemic value is the haven of those who lack Self, that is, intrinsic value, and it is hell for those who are living their inner Self, as tragedies from *Antigone* to *Dr. Zhivago* attest.

On the other hand, not all systemic valuation is evil. It is highly important and necessary. It is evil only when it is applied inappropriately and unintelligently to human situations.

J. Extrinsic Value

Analytic concepts derive from everyday empirical things and persons in space and time. We abstract – separate out – from all the chairs in the world, or all the girls in the world, or all the whatnots in the world those properties which are common. What we come up with, then, are the properties of the concept "chair," "girl," or "whatnot" (or "x").

In the degree that an analytic concept is fulfilled or not fulfilled, degrees of extrinsic valuation appear, ranging from goodness to fairness to poorness to badness.

The properties of such concepts are denumerable, that is, countable, one by one. For they have been abstracted one by one. A set of items which can be identified one by one is mathematically a denumerable set. Now how many properties can I abstract that things have in common? If I have a huge number of things, very few properties will be in common; if I have very few things, they will have very many properties in common and theoretically I can abstract common properties one by one *ad infinitum*.

The range of the number of properties that can be abstracted, then, is between one and infinity; that is, the properties of an analytic concept, are, at most, *denumerably* infinite. The mathematical sign for such an *actual* infinity is $\aleph_0$, which is the Hebrew $\aleph$ (aleph) with a zero at index, and must be distinguished from ∞, a potential, not actual, infinity. Potential infinity corresponds to the act of abstracting; actual infinity corresponds to the result of that act.

K. Intrinsic Value

Now let us consider the *singular concept*. When I think of my wife the way I should – not as a housekeeper or as a wife in comparison with other wives – she's unique. In that case the concept "my wife" is a singular concept. How many properties does she have? She has an infinity of properties, and I cannot really enumerate or define them. I see her, as the psychologists would say, as an uninterrupted whole or a "gestalt," or, as the mathematicians would say, as a "continuum." I neither abstract from nor define her. I live her life, identifying myself with her. I love her because she is as she is, not because she is better than another. She is, in other words, intrinsically valuable, which means that the properties she has are non-denumerably infinite (non-countable), and the mathematical symbol for this is $\aleph$.

Here we are dealing mathematically with transfinite numbers, and some most peculiar things happen. There are infinitely many rational numbers, 1,2,3,4.... There are also infinitely many odd numbers, 1,3,5,7.... This means that, infinitely speaking, there are as many odd numbers as there are odd and even numbers. The same would be true for even numbers. So the mathematical definition for a transfinite number is that *the part equals the whole.*

This is a most peculiar arithmetic, yet in its field it is as exact as any other. Actually, it is much simpler than finite arithmetic. Suppose you add an infinity to an infinity, what is the result? Well, an infinity. Subtract an infinity from an infinity and – this is most significant – the result is still an infinity. Subtraction is not possible in infinite arithmetic. The only change that can happen is a rise to higher infinities by exponentiation, $\aleph_0{}^{\aleph_0} = \aleph_1$, and so on up to $\aleph_\aleph$, which if axiologically analyzed has all the properties theology ascribes to God.

'I,' too, is a singular concept. Each of my thoughts may be an infinity, for I think of this chair, I can think of my thinking of this chair, I can think of my thinking of my thinking of this chair, and so on ad infinitum. If I can have a denumerable infinity of thoughts – as potentially I can – then the infinity of this infinity is non-denumerable, for $\aleph_0{}^{\aleph_0} = \aleph_1$, intrinsic value.

This is the third proof of the infinity of the Self. It is an objective definition of the value of a human being.

Depending on how I fulfill the many infinite aspects of my Self in actuality, I am a good or not-good human being, and since moral good is the application of intrinsic value to human beings, the goodness in question is *moral goodness.*

The more properties a concept has, the higher is its value. A systemic value fulfills a concept of only n (a finite number of) properties, an extrinsic value a concept of at most $\aleph_0$ properties (a denumerable infinity of properties), but an intrinsic value fulfills a concept of at least $\aleph_1$ properties (a non-denumerable infinity of properties). It follows that intrinsic value is richer in properties than extrinsic value, and extrinsic value is richer in properties than systemic value.

Man may be defined in four ways: (1) as a rational being, (2) as the being who has his own definition of himself within himself, (3) as "the mirror of all things," (Pico della Mirandola), and (4) as "the self-actualizing being" (Kierkegaard). All four definitions lead axiologically to the same result: the infinite intrinsic value of the human individual.

Thus, compared to the value of the human Personality, the value of the entire extrinsic world is infinitely small and the value of a thought system is infinitely small. Yet it is easy to overvalue this infinitesimal value and to blow up an idea to mean the whole of existence – to make a fetish of it, to become a fanatic about it. Most of the great evil in history has been committed in the name of such an overvaluation.

Calvin caused Servetus to be burned at the stake over a slow fire as a heretic, but Castellio, in his imperishable protest, declared: "To burn a man alive does not defend a doctrine, but slays a man...We do not testify to our own faith by burning another, but only by our readiness to be burned on behalf of our faith." I think the same thing might be said of the collective incineration of men, women, and children by nuclear bombs.

Throughout history, unfortunately, wars, religious inquisitions, and such inhuman institutions as slavery have been justified in the name of God. My father was doing what he thought was something spiritual when he went gloriously forth to war in 1914. We try to satisfy our spiritual hunger in strange ways and get into trouble unless our scheme of values comes clear and true within us. The danger is that if we pour infinity into a thing or an idea, we are likely to disvalue the human person. *It is the person who has the highest value, because only the person is of infinite worth.*

Value conflicts on this intrinsic or spiritual level can only be resolved in favor of the person. I love my wife, and I love my philosophy, and the two go nicely together, but should there be a conflict, then the person takes absolute precedence. That's all there is to it. Oddly enough, *my own philosophy has taught me the relative unimportance of my philosophy.* Suppose you are a husband who works for a corporation. When everything is normal and there's no emergency, then there's no conflict. When the corporation has an emergency and your wife is normal, the corporation takes precedence. When the corporation is normal and your wife has an emergency, your wife takes precedence. When both the corporation and your wife have emergencies, then there's absolutely no doubt about it from a value point of view. Your wife takes precedence.

3. The Application

Axiologists carry out scientific measurements of value with the aid of a calculus which arises by combining in every possible way the three value dimensions – systemic, extrinsic, intrinsic – and their respective value measurements – n, $\aleph_0$ and $\aleph_1$.

This calculus is based on the axiological fact that the most valuable value, *the value that fulfills the concept "value" most fully, is intrinsic value.* Any movement away from intrinsic value is negative; any movement toward it is positive.

The combinations of value can be either *compositions* or *transpositions.* A composition of values is a positive valuation of one dimension of value by another; a transposition is a negative valuation of one dimension by another.

Such compositions and transpositions can be systematized and symbolized, using "S" for systemic, "E" for extrinsic, and "I" for intrinsic. The birth of a baby, a religious experience, or a creative act, for example, would be a composition of the first value rank and would be symbolized I^I (an intrinsic valuation of an intrinsic value). The mixing of chocolate and sawdust, a car crash (one car wrecking another), or an explosion would be a transposition, a disvalue, and would be symbolized "E_E" – an extrinsic disvaluation of an extrinsic value. (The symbols "I^I" and "E_E" mean, respectively:

$$\aleph_1{}^{\aleph_1} = \aleph_2; \ \aleph_0{}_{\aleph_0} = \frac{1}{\aleph} \quad).$$

The combinations of value can in turn be combined, producing secondary, tertiary, quaternary, etc., compositions and transpositions. A quaternary value combination is one with five elements, such as $(E_S)^I)_I)^S$. This symbolizes, for example, a personal experience I had in Mexico. A highway patrolman stopped me. As an element of a system, the patrolman, S, disvalued my driving, E, producing this transposition, E_S. My wife, who felt all along I was driving too fast, thoroughly enjoyed the situation, $(E_S)^I$; I thoroughly disliked her enjoyment of it, $(E_S)^I)_I$, and the patrolman relished the whole situation by giving me a ticket, $(E_S)^I)_I)^S$. There are 3,888 different forms of such quaternary value situations, and each form may mean an infinity of such situations. Thus E_S may also symbolize my opinion that my soldier's uniform is a systemic disvaluation of a good piece of clothing. Someone else may feel differently and regard it as E^S, the systemic valuation of an ordinary piece of clothing. My girl friend likes my uniform greatly $(E_S)^I$, her father dislikes her liking it $(E_S)^I)_I$, and the commanding officer likes the situation, in the name of the army and of a soldier's love $(E_S)^I)_I)^S$. Here we have the stuff of an operetta in our formula.

Of quinary value forms (involving six elements) there are 23,328, each again applicable to an infinite number of situations. At the National University of Mexico, an automatic computer is now being programmed for more than a billion value situations. When completed, it will be axiology's "table of logarithms" and will include 1,306,125,378 value patterns to which the axiological scientist may refer in calculating his measurements.

This gives, of course, a greatly condensed view of the possibilities formal axiology holds for the use of value X-rays in human situations. We are at the rudimentary beginnings. With the practice of axiology begins the new science of valuation. The creation of the system is only the structure which enables us, as it were, to climb to the plateau. Before us stretches the new horizon. Formal axiology, to be a genuine science, must be applicable to the whole vast panorama of the realm of values.

The task before us is to include more and more ethical as well as moral phenomena and to map out systematically the new realm. The axiological system itself must be elaborated and expanded. The border lines between the various value realms – the moral, aesthetic, religious, economic, etc. –

must be drawn with precision. All this must be done systematically and consistently, employing the new instrument of value science. In the future it may well be that social scientists will have to learn axiology just as today physicists and chemists learn mathematics.

In general, the applications of the value dimensions –systemic, extrinsic, intrinsic – to the various fields of human activity will produce the various social and moral sciences. Consider these examples. Extrinsic value applied to individual persons yields the science of Psychology. Intrinsic value applied to individual persons yields the science of Ethics. Systemic value applied to individual persons yields the science of Physiology. These and other applications of the three dimensions of value are shown in the accompanying table.

AXIOLOGICAL SCIENCES

APPLIED TO:	INTRINSIC VALUE	EXTRINSIC VALUE	SYSTEMIC VALUE
INDIVIDUAL PERSONS	Ethics	Psychology	Physiology
GROUPS OF PERSONS	Political Science, Social Ethics	Sociology	Law of Persons
INDIVIDUAL THINGS	Aesthetics	Economics	Technology
GROUPS OF THINGS	Civilization	Ecology	Industrial Technology, Civil Engineering, Games, Law of Property, Ritual
CONCEPTS	Metaphysics	Epistemology	Logic
GOD	Mysticism	Comparative Religion	Theology
WORDS	Poetry	Rhetoric	Grammar

Such applications to actual situations are a vast task for new generations of pure and applied axiologists, pure and applied social and moral scientists and, finally, the mechanics and craftsmen of social and moral situations.

Already, however, formal axiology is being used to measure the value of speeches by national and world leaders, of poems and plays, of court decisions, of newspaper and magazine articles, of moral conflicts. It is being used to value-analyze job applicants. It is being used to assess corporate programs and policies and to develop corporate manpower. It is being applied in anthropology. Perhaps most important, it is being used to help persons find meaning in their lives, by the persons themselves and by psychotherapists.

In business one can think immediately of many needs for axiological X-ray. Take the idea of a worker. Systemically, a worker is a production unit, valued in time and motion studies. Extrinsically, a worker is one of a number of workers performing this, that, or the other function. This calls for incentives and leads to different kinds of compensation. Intrinsically, a worker is a human being with infinite value, and this again leads to entirely different consequences, such as the partnership of worker and employer in profit-sharing.

Take an insurance agent or any other salesman. Systemically, he may be a functional being who has learned a certain 1, 2, 3 approach by rote. He follows that system and he sells – performs a function. Extrinsically, he has been trained to analyze situations and to use psychology; this, too, enables him to sell. But intrinsically he uses no set approach at all; he ignores all the rules and he runs away with the sales trophies. His secret: he identifies himself with his customer.

For that matter, every job has its systemic, extrinsic, and intrinsic potential. Take the president of a company. Systemically, he just pushes the right buttons (or vice presidents) and things go in there and come out here. His company's employees are like troops, and his customers (too often) are the enemy to be overcome. Extrinsically, he performs as a master politician, economic strategist, and capital stock manipulator in competition with other presidents of other companies. Intrinsically, however, his company's employees – and customers, too – are human beings, like himself, and he is concerned as to what effect his company's actions will have on them as people. So all his executive decisions are fraught with "intangibles," with human values that call for axiological measurement.

The human factor was dramatically revealed in the Hawthorne productivity tests. A group of factory girls were given better working conditions, and productivity increased. Then the improvements were taken away from them, but productivity still increased. The girls got mid-morning breaks and a shortened work week, and productivity increased. The breaks were eliminated and the work week lengthened, still productivity increased. No matter what was done, productivity went up. Roethlisberger and Dickson, the men conducting the research, were puzzled and wondered what kind of logic was at work here. They concluded: What is done is not so important; what is really important is the human attention given the girls and the cooperation they give in return. In other words, intrinsic valuation was mobilized; they were made aware of their humanity. The only thing that could happen was multiplication – increased productivity. The finite arithmetic of subtraction simply won't apply in such a situation.

Rest periods are another example of intrinsic valuation. Say you are considering rest periods of 20 minutes a day for your employees. Your time and motion engineers use their slide rules. "Twenty minutes a day less for 1,000 people is 20,000 minutes less a day, 100,000 minutes less a week, half a million minutes less work a month. You'll lose production." But you go ahead and introduce the rest periods anyway, and production *increases*. Again, what has happened? You went from extrinsic to intrinsic valuation; finite arithmetic, the arithmetic of substraction, passed out of the picture.

There are many more such examples. But let me tell you what happened to one of my students at the Massachusetts Institute of Technology. It illustrates rather strikingly, I think, that you don't have to wait for another generation; you don't need to know transfinite arithmetic; you don't need a computer; you can start to work right now applying some of the basics of value science for yourself, for situations you are in in the world, and for situations the world is in.

The semester had started in October, and in December we reached intrinsic value in our study of axiology. I asked the students to write term papers analyzing any situation or text they wanted to in terms of formal axiology. One, the editor of the college magazine, analyzed his own articles and found much more in them than he had ever thought was there. Another analyzed "The Cocktail Party" by T. S. Eliot; a third, *Life* magazine editorials. One boy came to me just before classes broke for Christmas and said, "Sir, I want you to know that the writing of this paper is the most important thing in my life." I said, "How do you mean?" He said, "You must wait until you get my paper."

After the Christmas vacation I got the paper. It was entitled "Homecoming of a Son," and the story was this: He was a bright young fellow, on a four-year scholarship at MIT. His parents were Polish immigrants, and he was ashamed that they were just workers in a light bulb factory. Learning value science, however, he came to know clearly what he had only sensed vaguely: that a person is who he is, that it isn't so important what he does, and that his parents were wonderful persons. So he wanted to go home and tell them he loved them. But how could he do that without showing them at the same time that he had not loved them before? The paper told how he did it. He just produced one value situation after another and poured love into it. The whole household changed; laughter and happiness prevailed; it was an entirely new family.

It was a wonderful thing to read this paper, like a miracle consciously brought about. Then, after about three weeks he came into my office with a letter from his mother. "John," she wrote him, "this was a beautiful and strange vacation, and Dad and I have been thinking about it and talking about it all this time and finally we have come to a conclusion. We want you to know our conclusion. *It is that we had never loved you before*...Life is sure funny, isn't it? You go through the years while life is passing you by thinking you are doing what's right, and yet you are blind to what really is happening around you."

Now just reflect upon what happened here. Nobody talked to anybody about what was going on, yet the logic of value worked itself out to such a degree that the parents could put into words, from their point of view, what the boy had started out to accomplish in the first place. Love had been missing – as it is also missing in so much of the world today – but it was there now in an entirely new world brought about by what they described as a strange and beautiful vacation.

In many similar ways it should be possible for every one of us to use value science in our own lives, without calculus, and without complicated formulae. We need only learn how to apply the yardstick of intrinsic value to life around us and within us.

In the following chapters, I'll be discussing this kind of personal use of formal axiology. First, how do you go about sensitizing and developing your Self? Second, how does value science appear in your religion? Third, how can you apply value science in evaluating the international nuclear crisis?

Chapter Three

GEORGE'S – AND EVERYONE'S – PROBLEM

We have defined goodness – anything is good when it has all the properties it's supposed to have – and we've built a scientific axiology around that axiom.

With this science we have found that we can know and measure value in its systemic, extrinsic (social), and intrinsic (Self or spiritual) dimensions, and we've found that a human life in its infinity is the most valuable thing there is.

We have, I believe, laid the foundations for the organization of goodness and peace in the world.

But it's all, of course, much easier said than done. It's still up to individual human beings to help themselves and the world recover from this sickness unto death. It's one thing to agree with Kierkegaard that most of us live only in the basements of our houses; it's quite another thing to bestir ourselves sufficiently to move upstairs.

Indeed, Kierkegaard goes on to say:

> Men...have for the most part a very lowly conception of themselves, that is to say, they have no conception of being spirit, the absolute of all that a man can be...Not only does a man prefer to dwell in the cellar; he loves that to such a degree that he becomes furious if anyone would propose to him to occupy the *bel étage* which stands empty at his disposition – for in fact he is dwelling in his own house...[5]

Yet man *does* yearn to be better than he is, to be truly himself. The divine does persist within; but we are torn this way and that. Social and business pressures push us, and we go along, but the spark within is hard to extinguish, and even as we hurry to conform we may pause to wonder if this is all there is to life, and we glance uneasily over our shoulders (once a week or more), wondering vaguely if we haven't forgotten something, a cheerful word perhaps, a quiet moment, a little love – could it possibly be ourselves we have forgotten?

Something like this, I think, must have been bothering Bill Russell, the great center of the champion professional Boston Celtics basketball team, when he told a sports writer, "Maybe you'll think I'm a funny guy, but I don't feel what I'm doing is really important. I don't feel fulfilled. What I'd really like to do is discover something or invent something I'd be proud to tell my children."

I have a feeling that because of the threat of nuclear catastrophe which today hangs over us all, there is more secret longing for inner, spiritual strength today than ever before in man's history. *The need for spiritual growth is the greatest human need there is.* Satisfaction of that need is vital to mankind, I think, for it points the way out of our spiritual chaos and toward that realm of infinite human love which can be man's destiny, "a little lower than the angels."

It is this spiritual yearning, I'm sure, that causes so many executives, management men, and students to ask me, in effect, "How can I get hold of this thing, this inner power, and put it to work for me?" A member of one of my management development seminars put it like this:

Talking with some of the others about what you've been telling us, I gather that what worries them the most is whether they can act the way they know they *should* act. George would like very much to be George, to be himself at work as well as at home, in whatever he does, to fulfill his definition of himself, as you've said. George has so long been accustomed to acting like someone else – his boss's conception of George, for example – that it's really quite something for him even to consider acting like himself. Still, he fears that if he does become really George, his boss won't like it, and he'll lose his chance for a raise, or promotion – he might even lose his job. Now what's George to do?

This man is saying, "What good does it do a person to know about all this potential inner strength he has if in practical, everyday situations he can't use it even if he knows how?"

This really is serious, I think, not only for George but for his company, for society, and for America. Among the personnel of every organization – business, social, political – lie great untapped inner resources for innovation, creativity, long- and wide-range planning, and human leadership – in a word, for good. Also in every organization arise the situations of stress and strain which can be handled properly only by individuals able to tap those inner resources.

The higher you go in management the more essential becomes the use of your inner Self, your spiritual power, because your decisions become increasingly loaded with moral and spiritual implications. Far too often you make decisions which you, if you are sensitive, can hardly stomach and would never make if it were not that you know you are expected to make them – it's your role – and you must make them if you are, say, to beat last year, beat that other sales region, win that trip to Bermuda, or win that promotion over Jones. It's estimated that management and social pressures and tensions which affect all workers account for a loss to industry every year of at least three billions of dollars because of job changes, absenteeism, alcoholism, interpersonal frictions, executive breakdowns, and other emotional difficulties. The *Harvard Business Review* reports that eighty percent of the executives who would talk about it admitted that unethical practices are a generally accepted practice in their respective industries. Every one of us, I have no doubt, knows personally of men who, under severe pressure and moral strain, have deserted their Selves and "cracked up" physically or mentally.

Such value crises do not occur only in business, of course; they happen in the home, in the church, in politics, in every part of our lives. What I have to say, then, applies not only to George at work but also, in much the same way, to George at home, George in church, and George as a citizen in his community.

It could be tragic if in America, of all places, one's freedom to develop himself intrinsically is stifled, if the individual, in the name of the systemic idols and extrinsic goals of a collective organization, is walled off from humanity, the pursuit of happiness, and God. The business man, the administrator, the politician, the worker, who, acting as a specialist, perhaps a "transportation specialist," violates human intrinsic value, fouls himself, fouls mankind, and fouls God. In a corporate civilization like ours, this is precisely the kind of thing that can mire us in economic determinism, Godless materialism not unlike that in Soviet Russia, and "sickness unto death." In the past decade American life has produced plenty of evidence that this can happen here. I need tick off only a few scandals to make my point: the TV quiz show frauds, the call girls used as business bait by prominent corporations, the Billie Sol Estes case, Bernard Goldfine and Sherman Adams, the college basketball briberies, the electrical equipment industry price conspiracy, the attempt to market the baby-deforming drug Thalidomide, the rise in crimes of violence (and the growing popularity of violence as a way of life), the increasing domination of life by the military, the increase in high school dropouts and juvenile delinquency, the prevalent attitude of disrespect for the law, the callousness toward unemployment, poverty, sickness, and racial injustice.

The danger arises, I think, from the growth of organizational bigness. The life of the Organization is apt to become more important than the life of the individual. George and Jim are likely to become loyal Organization servants first, human beings second; executives first, lovers, husbands, fathers, or real persons second. Even friendships are likely to depend entirely upon their extrinsic value to the Organization. In all this, human intrinsic values naturally would take a beating. The inner Self would be practically lost.

What can you do about it? Frankly, it's rough. There is no easy answer, but let me do my best to give axiological directions and guidelines.

Let me make it clear that George will have his problem primarily when his company – or his home – is run systemically, at the expense of the human element – when rules, procedures, regulations, and system prevail over people, when there is pressure, pressure, pressure to meet the quotas, and when the quotas are always being raised.

A company operated in this fashion is primarily a money-making machine, and, in my opinion, because it ignores people, it's a poor way to make money. Many businessmen would like to ignore people because they are so unreasonable and unpredictable, and this makes planning difficult. Indeed, it's been suggested that this may be one explanation for the current corporate popularity of the various management "games" where price and production decisions are made and results obtained based on those decisions, without interference from capricious consumers.

Nevertheless, men who know how to work with people are increasingly in demand in business. Surveys, indeed, indicate this quality is prized much more highly than technical skill in holders of upper echelon positions. Inability to cooperate with others and inability to judge people have been found to be two of the most frequent reasons for executive failure.

In business, as elsewhere, then, the human factor of intrinsic value is at work, and until computers and other machines take over completely, it cannot be ignored. We've seen this human factor at work in the previously mentioned Hawthorne experiments where special attention was given one group of girls, in properly conducted profit-sharing arrangements, and in the strange mathematics of the twenty-minute rest breaks. It reflects, in business, what is true in society as a whole. A nation that aspires only to material progress, says Historian Arnold J. Toynbee, is doomed to economic stagnation, boredom, and moral decay. No society, he insists, has ever flourished without a spiritual meaning. The same thing could be said about a man – after all, most mental cases result from dull, hopeless, meaningless lives – and the same thing could be said about a business, for a businessman needs spiritual meaning in what he does as much as anyone.

I was delighted to read this corroborating statement in an *Atlantic Monthly* article by Edward T. Chase[6] titled "Money Isn't Everything":

The degree to which a society turns away from the immediacy of money-making to the cultivation of the resources of the mind and spirit substantially determines its ultimate economic growth. This is a new concept in economics that has been proved statistically only in the past several years.

President Murray D. Lincoln of Nationwide Insurance has long been saying the same thing: "We've never gone into anything primarily with the idea of making money out of it, but somehow we nearly always seem to end up pretty well in that department, too."

Another prominent businessman told me that the more he concentrated on making money the less he made. This is quite understandable. For in concentrating on making money you do not concentrate on the element which alone makes moneymaking possible – the needs of human beings. There are, as I have mentioned, numerous instances of salesmen who break all the rules but run away with the sales trophies because they are genuinely aware of their customers, they love to do things for people, and their sincerity is recognized as authentic, not artificial. I was told about an insurance agent with qualities like these. He's the rookie in a district force of a dozen agents, and he flunked some of his early assignments, but now he leads the district in sales production by a wide margin. Why? Here's what one of his colleagues says:

> This man has something within him. I can't pin it down, but I know what others have said. A minister: "This man walks with God." A friend: "He's just naturally loved by everyone." His wife: "As long as he's doing for others, he's happy." Everyone understands this agent like ABC.

An executive told me about his father, who ran a small tavern near New York City. He was very unbusinesslike. When his son came home from out of town for a visit one night, he hustled the customers out and closed up, several hours early. When family friends arrived at home one noon, he walked out, leaving the customers to fend for themselves until he returned. "Don't worry," he said. "They'll put the money for their drinks in the drawer." His place was a hangout for Brooklyn Dodger fans. During a baseball world series, a stranger came in, ordered a beer. "Who you for?" he was asked. "I'm for the Yankees," the man said. "Friend," the tavern owner told him, "you have this one on the house and then you better leave. We don't want no Yankees around here. There might be trouble." Ill health forced him to sell out his lively and prosperous little business. Within six months the new owner had gone broke for lack of customers.

There is, believe me, an intrinsic value side to business.

An economic act, a mere "fact" in the world of business, transcends itself and is embedded in a wider context. Gilbert K. Chesterton, the English writer, used to say that when he looked for a room he didn't look for the hot and cold water, the plumbing or furniture, but for the landlady's views of the universe. Even in the economic realm, intrinsic value precedes the extrinsic, and the moral or human context is more important than the economic.

But supposing you are a businessman who, to make a lot of money, deliberately sets out to operate on that top level – the moral or spiritual level. Your goal is to make profits, so you are nice to your employees and your customers, and you help the church. But that won't work because you have reversed the arrow. You have made the spiritual, the intrinsic, into a means to the economic. When you live truly spiritually, you cannot be thinking of material rewards at all. Every dollar that comes to you, you will shake your head in surprise and say, "I sure don't understand how it happened I got that one."

So back to George. If he's working with a company that is run almost entirely on the lower or systemic level, he won't get much encouragement in developing his true Self-potential; indeed, he'll be blocked and frustrated at every turn. He has three choices: (1) he can forfeit his individuality and become a cog in a machine that will from then on stamp out his life; (2) he can stay and try to help change things so that his company is run with the human concern paramount; or (3) if he regards the situation as utterly miserable and hopeless, he will have to consider leaving for self-employment or for another company or organization that does provide an environment favorable to Self-fulfillment.

Like everyone else, George is a unique individual of infinite intrinsic value; in my opinion he should let no organization smother his uniqueness and so disvalue him. For George, and for every person, the most important thing in the world is to fulfill his inner yearning – to achieve his unique Self-awareness and move up from the cellar.

Let's assume, then, that George's situation is not hopeless but hopeful. Let's assume that his company is run or could be run so as to permit him to develop his potentialities. What should he do to develop his inner Self, to live more on the intrinsic level, so that he can also live better on the systemic and extrinsic levels? For it is true, and it can be demonstrated axiologically, that the more fully we are ourselves, the better we can be at our jobs, in our social roles, and in our thinking. From our inner Self we get what it takes to be anything we want to be. Thus, Self-development is not a luxury; it is a necessity for our being truly ourselves on all three levels. So George's own inner being has to become part of his job. He has to live on the top (intrinsic) level in whatever he does, and he – George himself – has to do it; nobody else can live there for him.

But how? Again, in greater or lesser degree, at work or at home, this is everyone's problem.

1. Rules for Developing the Inner Self

First of all, I would say, you have to achieve clarity about yourself. Philosophers have tried to show you how to do it, from Socrates to Kierkegaard. What they have said can be synthesized into what I call the four Self rules.

The first is Socrates': *know thyself.* You (and George) have to find out what kind of person you are, what kind of properties you have, what kind of material has been given to you to live with.

The second is Kierkegaard's: *choose thyself.* This means that once you have found out what kind of person you are, you have to accept yourself and make the best of it because this is all you have. You have to choose yourself; you are your own material. This is the material you have to develop to infinity, and there is absolutely no limit, from the bottom at which you start to the height to which you can go. Jesus said to the thief who repented: "Today shalt thou be with me in Paradise." Mary Magdalene was a prostitute and became a saint; Matthew was a tax collector, which at that time meant a robber and collaborator with the Romans, and he became a writer of the Gospel. There is no limit to the lowness at which you may start. But no matter how despicable you may be to yourself, you must choose yourself, accept yourself as the one you are. "I am the one I am."

The third rule is Pico della Mirandola's and also Kierkegaard's: *create thyself.* Make yourself into the very best person you can. You are your own creation. It's never too late, but start as early as you can, and never stop. There is more joy in heaven for one sinner who repents than for ninety-nine just persons who need no repentance.

The fourth rule is Jesus': *give thyself.* This means forget all limitations, be generous with your own Self. Give your Self to your fellow man and to the world. Love your neighbor as you love yourself. Throw your bread upon the water. Lack of love is the cause of our trouble. If everyone would love himself and his neighbor, fear of war and violence would fade away. This is the Gospel truth, expressed both by Jesus and the Prophets, both in the Old Testament (Leviticus 19:18) and the New (Matthew 22:37-40). The *Bible* is one.

To love yourself and, within yourself, your fellow man is, thus, the end result of a chain of Self-discoveries, from Self-knowledge to Self-choosing to Self-creating to Self-giving. You can give yourself only when you have created yourself, when your own Self is no longer in your own way and you are intrinsically free. The more you grow transparently within yourself the more power you will find within – as if you had found the key to a treasure house. You will not only be able to love yourself, your wife, your family, life itself – you will find that your power to love is inexhaustible. Your love will become deeper and deeper, richer and richer, get ever new facets, so that what you call love today will appear like playing marbles tomorrow.

To achieve still more clarity about yourself, take the test which follows to find out where you stand in the development of your inner Self. The test lists the moral properties of the Man of Faith and the Man of Fear.

If you live in the depth of yourself you are a world for yourself and you need nothing else. You are anchored with the totality of your own being in the totality of the world. You feel at home in the world; you feel at ease. The strange thing is, everything comes to you without any special effort –

everything is added unto you, as it says in the *Bible*. You are, as we say, well born. You feel wonderful to be alive. Faith is exactly this – to feel good in the world and to feel that the world is good. You are not only made in the image of God and bear intrinsically His name – ("I am I") – but you also see the world with the eyes of God: "And God saw everything that He had made and, behold, it was very good" (Genesis 1:31). You are not letting God down by feeling the world is rotten. You have nothing spiritually to fear, for you have the deep trust that God is good and the world is His creation; and you have the humility, as did Job, to trust in the goodness of God and the world even though at times you are unable to understand either the one or the other.

2. Intrinsic Faith and Intrinsic Fear

Intrinsic Faith is the fundamental property of the morally good man.

On the other hand there is the unfortunate fellow who is not well born, who has not found himself, who has not anchored himself deeply within the world as a whole. That poor guy is ill-at-ease. He feels that his birth was an accident, that he is an error of the universe. He really should not have been born, he thinks. He does not like himself; he wishes he were not himself. He lives in spite of himself, and in spite of everything. He is defiant, intrinsically at odds with himself, with the whole world, and with God. God to him is not a beloved and trusted Father. He is a fearful and mistrusted master – as believed the unfaithful servant in the Parable of the Talents. This man lacks faith. His whole life is one of great doubt or fear. He knows not who he is or what he is up to. He is intrinsically bewildered and hence afraid.

Intrinsic Fear is the fundamental property of the morally insecure person.

These two great fundamental properties characterize two very different kinds of people: the morally secure and the morally insecure, the strong and the wobbly, the wideawake and the sleepy. St. Paul called them the aware ones and the wary ones. The man of Faith is a cosmic optimist. There are many bad things in the world, but they are flaws of the design or the execution of the world, not of its essence. They belong to the realm of contingency, a small part, a statistically calculable small part, of the grand design. The man of Fear is a cosmic pessimist. He sees all the bad things in life, all the suffering, and he says, "How is God possible with all this misery around? It would be blasphemy to believe in a God who created this world." He does not see the whole for the parts.

Now look at the properties that flow from the two fundamental moral types, the Man of Fear and the Man of Faith. I doubt whether you'll find that you are all one or the other, but you can learn which you most resemble.

THE MAN OF FEAR IS –

– *defiant*. He defies the whole world. He assumes he is superior to everyone. Because he lacks faith in the world, in anyone, he has to be the guy who does it all. He trusts only himself. He can't delegate. Everything depends upon him, for he thinks he is indispensable.

– *aggressive and combative*. He has to be because everything depends upon him.

– *competitive*. To him everyone is a potential rival or enemy who must be beaten or overcome. He has to be the top dog all the time.

– *cynical*. He has to tear down everyone and everything.

– *greedy*. Unless he grabs his, somebody else will get it. He has to keep piling it up, lest he may starve one day.

– *vain*. He feels the need of a lot of props for himself. The more columns he has in *Who's Who*, the better he feels. He builds his outer self. He looks in the mirror and his finery makes him feel good.

– *easily hurt, touchy*. He's so insecure, and he has great self-

THE MAN OF FAITH IS –

– *humble*. He bends to the spirit, not to man, so has no need for defiance or superiority. He doesn't have to pretend anything because he trusts God and knows everything will be all right.

– *serene*. He feels a deep joy at being alive and makes everyone around him feel the same way. He is spiritually happy.

– *cooperative*. He sees others as potential helpers in meeting problems. Everyone can be a friend.

– *humane*. He loves people. He helps them. He never says a bad word about anyone.

– *generous*. He knows he can afford to give because he knows that when he throws his bread on the water it will return to him manifold.

– *unpretentious*. He doesn't try to call attention to his appearance. He doesn't have to try to pretend he is anything but what he is. This is his world and he belongs.

– *self-possessed, not easily hurt*. He never expects anything extra

pity. He has to struggle so hard, and everything is against him. He's concerned only about his suffering, not that of others.

– *cowardly*. He is scared in his spirit, thin-skinned. He is born, so to speak, without a spiritual skin against the world, but he is sensitive only about himself. He is a spiritual crybaby; few things appear possible to him. He tries to hoard what he has – like the unfaithful servant in the Parable of the Talents.

– *burdened with the heavy touch*. Everything is very difficult for him. He has to work so hard, harder than anyone else, and nothing comes of it.

– *prone to see the irrelevant*. He lacks a sense of proportion, makes mountains out of mole hills, or vice versa. He thus confuses the important with the unimportant, and his thinking is irrelevant.

– *inconstant, hesitant*. He lacks enough faith and inner strength to move toward his objective consistently, so he has a certain deep hesitation about his actions. He goes to a certain point, then stops, looking for another direction.

– *systemic, rigid*. He uses systems as a crutch and is lost without them – as was Adolf Eichman. The system is sovereign over him.

from the world, but he takes whatever he receives as a gift from the bounty of God's goodness, for which he is grateful.

– *bold, courageous*. Nothing appears impossible, every problem seems solvable, every difficulty superable. He knows he is on the right track so he isn't afraid to move ahead.

– *blessed with the light touch*. He bounces through life, buoyed by the powers of infinity. Everything comes easy to him.

– *prone to see the relevant*. He has a sense of proportion, sees things in their true relation to each other. He is able to differentiate. He takes the important seriously and values it accordingly.

– *persevering, patient*. He knows he's on the right road and if he persists, he will reach his goal, he feels within himself the strength of the universe. He is still water that runs deep.

– *spontaneous, flexible*. He plays upon and with systems as a virtuoso with a piano. He is sovereign above the system.

– indifferent, callous. He is indifferent toward what really counts, especially toward the infinite greatness of the human being. Since he is weak inside and hates to be touched by anything unpleasant, he is indifferent to suffering.

– compassionate. Compassion is his deepest trait. He suffers with the sufferer. Every suffering is his own. He manifests within himself the intrinsic oneness of all Creation. Compassion, as we said, is the touchstone of morality.

As I said, none of us, of course, has all the properties of either the Man of Faith or the Man of Fear. We are all mixtures. I have trouble with a number of the fearful man's properties. For example, superiority. I used to think I was the most important guy in creation. Now I'm not so sure. Even so, my wife has to keep reminding me, "Be humble." I know a fellow who is an engineer, one of the most lovable persons I know. He has many of the properties of faith, but he also has a deep-seated, intrinsic fear. He lacks serenity, is often on the defensive, is not expansive but narrow, and is easily hurt. Actually, he is extremely successful in a material way, with a beautiful home and a garage full of Cadillacs. But he is always fearful he will lose all he has tomorrow. He feels he's no good; he shouldn't have been born; life isn't really worth the trouble. If the Bomb does away with us all, that's all right with him. He's not worried. Yet he's very much afraid of losing his money. You cannot say this is a bad man, but he is morally insecure; he has not developed the totality, the depth, the infinity within himself. Value logic requires all people, good or bad, to judge goodness and badness in their own image, and to use the same words for goodness and badness. As a result a stingy person will find another stingy person good and a generous person bad, a prodigal. In general someone who lives on the systemic and extrinsic levels (on the left side of the Table) will find a person on the intrinsic level (on the right side) not as he is – authentic, unpretentious, generous, etc. – but rather vain, stingy, competitive, tricky, etc. Such adjectives and much worse were applied to Abraham Lincoln. Thus, it makes a tremendous difference who says what. I was hired once because a fellow said I was no good. Person A asked Person B about this man Hartman. And Person B said he's no good. But Person A had a poor opinion of Person B. So he figured that if Person B said Hartman is no good, Hartman must really be a humdinger. And he hired me.

Now undoubtedly, as I have said, unless you are a paragon, you will see that you don't measure up to some properties of the Man of Faith. You may note uneasily the respects in which you do not fulfill your Self-definition. You are perhaps too little aware, too aggressive, too vengeful, too cynical, or, like me, too superior. What do you do to shuck off the fearful properties and develop the faithful ones? In other words, we're back to the main question, "How do we become Self-aware?"

I've already given a partial answer. You have to know there is something within you which is intrinsically unique and extremely valuable to you, to the universe, and to God. You have to know that you make use of only a fraction of that spiritual power. You have to *know* thyself, *choose* thyself, create thyself, give thyself. You have to know that full development of yourself intrinsically takes a lifetime.

This Self-development is what makes you Yourself. Only you can give your Self firmness, certainty, and moral security. You are at rest only when you have the world in your Self and do not need to hunt for it in all kinds of hustle and bustle. Physically you're only a little person on a huge globe, but within you, you can, if you fulfill your Self, contain the whole world, all humanity, indeed the vastness of the universe and God.

Let's analyze this Self-development, this growth process of the 'I.' The 'I' that I am within myself is not static; it is dynamic. The concept that 'I am I' is the core of my being. At birth I am given body, mind, and emotion – the capacity for feeling good, bad, pleasant, angry, etc. As a baby I'm a little animal. I have not such mind. I don't think. I am a little body, and my first actions are to get acquainted with my body. I look at myself, stick my toes into my mouth, smell myself, and so on. It's nearly two years before I speak of myself, saying 'I.' That's a wonderful moment. Parents do not celebrate it as they ought. It is the combination of the process of the growth of self-reflection from the animal to the human. (Psychoanalysts tell us that this process begins in the second month of the child's life with the first smile.)

This process is one of qualitative growth. Quantitative growth is no problem; I just grow. But qualitative growth is different; it is the growth of meaning. Let me illustrate. A sculptor has before him a big block of marble. As such, it has little meaning; it's just a block of marble. The sculptor chisels around this block and sometimes chisels off more than he leaves, but at the end there is a beautiful statue. *Moses*, by Michelangelo, let's say. The meaningless block of marble with a minimum of material has acquired maximum meaning.

That's an example of qualitative growth. It's throwing away what isn't meaningful and differentiating, while liberating and refining what's left over. Michelangelo sometimes walked around a block of marble for years before he began chiseling away at it. In his mind, or rather his person, he then had the final product, and he had to get it out of that marble. So the 'I' is the sculptor. The material – the marble – is body, mind, and feeling, and I have to make out of the material given to me a work of art, a work of meaning. In other words, I have to peel away the animality of my body, the irrelevant of the mind, the disturbing of the emotion and make myself, as Kierkegaard says, more and more transparent (like glass), less and less obstructive to the 'I,' the inner Self. For example, if, when I try to talk to you, I stutter, my physical mouth is an obstruction to my inner meaning and I have to overcome it. Suppose my thoughts are unclear. I have to clear them up. Suppose I'm very emotional, or not emotional enough. Everything has to serve and become my meaning; that is qualitative growth.

I can grow qualitatively in many ways. I can become an artist, a sculptor, an insurance man. I can be anything as long as I make myself into something more than I am materially given. In other words I have to transcend my material being, and I have to give myself transcendent meaning. I must become a symbol for something higher. If I am a good salesman, I will live and breathe my job; I will transcend my physical body and live in the person of my customer. If you were to ask me how I do it, I wouldn't be able to tell you. Salesmen are given courses in economics and psychology which they learn forward and backward, but there's always that one, like the rookie agent somebody said "walks with God," who breaks all the rules and makes the most sales. Qualitative growth. The deepening of meaning.

3. Six Ways to Self-development

Again, how? Assuming that neither you nor George has reached the point where you might require psychotherapy, I'm going to suggest six ways that can lead to Self-development.

1. One way is to take seriously the teachings of your *religion*. Become, in other words, a truly religious person intrinsically, not just an extrinsic member of a church. "Love God. Love thy neighbor as thyself. Overcome evil by good." I'll elaborate in the next chapter.

2. Another way is through *crisis*. In crisis a deep sickness, the loss of a beloved, or some other traumatic experience – we are forced to delve deeply to find our strength. This is a pretty rough way to Self-development, and it cannot be brought about voluntarily. When crisis strikes, we may just as easily go under as triumph. It may break us rather than make us. We have to throw away our finite life and leap into the abyss. We have to throw our Self at the mercy of God. A great example of Self-development through crisis was that of Franklin D. Roosevelt, from the day he was stricken with polio at Campobello on August 10, 1921, to the day, June 26, 1924, when at Madison Square Garden he nominated Al Smith as the Democratic Presidential candidate – standing on his own two legs, holding the podium with his left hand, and waving with his right hand to the screaming, cheering crowd, a man triumphantly emerged from the depth of despair to a new life. After his Campobello crisis, Roosevelt said, "What I called thinking yesterday was merely looking out of the window."

3. A third way is through a conscious, deliberate effort to refine your sensibilities, to sensitize and develop your *conscience* so that you know evil or good when you see it. Make that voice so strong you cannot compromise. In Mexico two boys were driving one rainy evening to Acapulco. There was suddenly a thud, and something like a body went flying through the air. The driver kept right on. His companion said, "Stop, man, stop, you've hit someone!" "Oh," said the driver, "never mind that. He shouldn't have been in the road." But his companion became so hysterical the driver backed up. They got out and there was a woman sitting there crying, a little boy in her arms. He was injured, but not fatally. In such a situation, the driver obviously was insensitive to human life; he was without compassion. His friend, whom I later had as a student and who told me the story, turned out to be the opposite.

One way to develop your conscience is to follow the example of sensitive persons like a Maria, like a child, like your wife. A wife who loves is usually more mature than a man. She loves you as a husband, not as an important or not-so-important man, and she may love you when you're asleep more than at any other time. To women, both the intellectual and – if true women – the social play small roles relative to love and compassion. Men are often lured by their intellectual and social power to insensitivity and disregard of the spiritual. Having to deal directly with the creation of life, women are usually more sensitive to intrinsic value.

Conscience is the organ of the Self. It is, so to speak, the barometer of the soul, the measure of its spiritual pressure. In the degree that we register normal sensitivity, especially compassion, our conscience is sensitive; in the degree that we do not, it is insensitive and undeveloped. In our conscience we register the properties of the Man of Faith and the Man of Fear, and it's good to check this spiritual barometer.

4. A fourth way to Self-development is by using your *intellectual power*. You can develop yourself morally by learning intellectually about your Self and growing in step with your knowledge, and by mixing honest-to-goodness efforts to define and become your Self. But you must really work at it, 24 hours a day, as hard as men like Galileo and Newton worked at their problems. You work at it until one day something will snap, and this is it. You've experienced something like it when you learned to drive a car, or to speak a foreign language. Something clicked, and suddenly you drove or spoke. Psychologically this is called the "A-ha" experience. There is an "A-ha" experience on all levels, and the highest level is God. But you don't have to have it on that level. Have it on your own level; *be your own "A-ha" experience.* Make your own Self your problem; when you work hard at it you will suddenly find the just-right solution. You will find your self – and you will feel "A-ha." Any "A-ha" experience is a minute mystic experience.

The "A-ha" experience of finding your Self is not so minute, however; it puts you on the road to divinity.

It is the intellectual way to Self-development that I have taken, though I was helped profoundly by the crisis experience which expanded my awareness at one almost shattering stroke. Yet it was my lifelong endeavor to find a rational account of this experience, and I did find it eventually through the precision of formal axiology.

5. A fifth way to Self-development is through the conscious pursuit of *peak experiences.* A peak experience, in the terminology of Abraham Maslow, who has studied this subject intensively, is one in which we feel ourselves at the peak of life, in the fullness of our powers and the maximum depth of our awareness. It can come to us in love, in the birth of a child, the marriage of a son or daughter, in deep musical and other aesthetic experiences, in creation and inspiration, or in religious insight and rapture. Some persons can make their whole lives into a series of peak experiences. They work at their Being and not primarily at their doing, at their awareness rather than their activities. Their eye for knowledge gradually becomes sharper for the things that matter and weaker for the things that don't. They fulfill the prayer that Kierkegaard put as motto to his *The Sickness Unto Death.*

> Give us weak eyes, oh God,
> For things that matter not,
> And eyes of light and clarity
> For all thy truth and verity.

6. A sixth way to Self-development is to ask yourself the following four questions, and, after you've thought hard about them, come up with answers that satisfy you.

A. WHAT AM I HERE FOR IN THE WORLD?

In Mexico City I am with a personnel selection firm which tests candidates for executive positions. In interviews I ask the candidates this question, and I get some queer replies that really aren't answers at all. These men seem nonplussed, as if they had never heard such a foolish question before, and they go through tortuous maneuvers trying to figure out just what kind of answer will please me. Many come out with such answers as "To make a living," "To be happy," "To make money to support my family," or the Sunday school reply, "To complete my mission," without having the least idea what that might be.

What, then, *am* I here for in the world? To be a good, loyal company man? To do what I'm told? Well, no dog would lick me for that. To make a lot of money? Money can be a fetish. It's nice to have but not so important that I have to regard moneymaking as my main reason for being. You see, this takes us right back to the Self-definition question, "Who am I?". My answer is that I'm here to define and give meaning to myself. To give meaning to myself, I am trying to enrich the universe by articulating as clearly as possible the science of value, by helping to organize goodness, by making peace possible. This is my answer, not yours. You must find your own answer, and it will be the more true the more fully you are yourself. For then you will conclude that you represent divine capital and that you were born to make this capital grow and produce. The higher your meaning, the greater enrichment you will feel you have to offer the universe, and the more you have to develop your body and mind. The larger your meaning, the larger your life. It comes to mean complete dedication of your total Self to your task, using your body and mind for a meaning beyond yourself. You then transcend yourself. You become a symbol for a meaning beyond yourself. When I write this symbol – "City" – you don't think of the curves and angles of the lines, you think of the meaning of it – streets, houses, stores, people. You hardly see the letters. They don't obstruct. They are transparent, and they are transcendent. But if I write ρολις, the Greek word for city, you are stuck with the lines and curves of the symbol itself. It obstructs you.

If you aren't transparent, if you can't read your own symbol, you get in your own way; you don't understand your Self; you are, so to speak, "Greek" to your Self, Self-alienated. So you must make your body, mind, and spirit meaningful; your name must become a symbol of meaning. You must have the feeling that you are here for a reason. If you have that feeling, you have intrinsic depth; if you don't have it, well, then, you have to develop it.

One comment: greatness of meaning does not necessarily make us better morally than, say, Maria, who fully gives herself to a small, limited meaning. Breadth of meaning is what counts, not width; quality, not quantity. Maria could say that she is here in the world to clean houses, and that doesn't seem to have much meaning, but she puts into every action what Kierkegaard calls the motions of eternity. It is not what you do that counts, but the spirit in which you do it. You have it within you to fill a particular place in the world. If you move toward that place, large or small, great or not-so-great, then you have the feeling of meaning, of transparency. The point is that if you like what you are doing, you can begin to see it – no matter how humble – in the framework of eternity, and there you are on the first (intrinsic) level.

It's true that most people go through life without finding the answer to that question. What is so amazing, though, is that many of them have the answer in their lives but they don't see that they have it; they let it pass by unconsciously. Perhaps we need trained axioanalysts who would listen to life stories and tell persons the meanings of their lives.

B. WHY DO I WORK FOR THIS ORGANIZATION?

If I don't have any particular meaning in life, it really doesn't matter, of course, what or whom I work for. I just settle back and, working as well as living on a lower level, I just learn to classify, to put things in order, to manipulate and operate. In other words I become a specialist who sees only to the tip of his nose. My answer to the question would likely be a short one: to make money. In this case I make a living but I don't live; my life has no meaning. If, on the other hand, my life does have meaning for me, I will be quite concerned about the organization I work for, because it would have to dovetail with my own meaning. If it doesn't and I keep on working for it, I'm either a fake or unhappy or both. I cheat myself. I waste the divine capital that I am. I sell myself to the world, and I will pay for this betrayal by neurosis, by drinking too much, or by otherwise destroying myself, as if I were saying that I am not worth the gift of life.

C. WHAT CAN THIS ORGANIZATION DO TO HELP ME FULFILL MY MEANING IN THE WORLD?

This question implies, in other words, that the company I work with exists for me. This is true. An organization never rises above the individual person, because an organization cannot live on the intrinsic level. A company can systematically state intrinsic spiritual objectives, but individual persons have to fulfill those objectives. The company, therefore, has to be an instrument of my meaning. It has to be an extension of my Self, as are my body and mind, and like them must not obstruct my Self. It has to nourish my inner Self, give my spirit strength and sustenance – it has to be transparent to my meaning.

Many problems can arise here, and conscience perhaps has to work overtime. I was once in a situation which became so bad for me that I could not go into the same room with my superior without feeling nauseated. I was unhappy and depressed, my work suffered and I suffered, until at length I became physically ill and had to have an operation. Finally, there was nothing for me to do but get out, for my work no longer had meaning.

There are times when the only thing that counts is to be true to your Self, no matter what the consequences, when you have to take your life in your hands and run. This is when you need Faith and Boldness.

D. HOW CAN I HELP THIS ORGANIZATION FULFILL MY MEANING IN THE WORLD?

I, with all my power and good will, can reciprocate the good will of the organization toward me. For if the organization helps me to fulfill my purpose, I certainly will want to contribute one hundred percent of myself instead of holding back forty percent – as studies have shown the average worker does – and hurting myself as well as the company. I fulfill myself by fulfilling my duties, and more, toward the organization. It thus becomes the creative instrument of my own Self-fulfillment. There is no happier relationship than such a one toward and with a company with which you work.

These, then, are the four questions. They can be answered flippantly. What am I here for in the world? To make a living. Why do I work for this organization? To make money. What can this organization do to help me fulfill my purpose in the world? Pay me. How can I help this organization help me fulfill my purpose in the world? Help it to make more money.

These are answers on the extrinsic level; they are without value compared to those on the intrinsic level. It has been my experience that no executive can do his best unless he answers these questions on the intrinsic level and unless he puts into management jobs persons who can also answer them on that level. Such an executive integrates his life, his job, and his intellectual and spiritual interests into one; his mind stretches, his horizon widens, his vision lengthens; he acquires the foresight to plan far ahead, seeing his organization in a broadened context, in the light of long-term rather than short-term goals. With the maturing of sensitivity he also acquires the ability to plumb the intrinsic depths of persons who work with him and to articulate ways for their Self-development. He uses a new kind of logic to provide human incentives as well as material incentives. He becomes, indeed, a harmonious human being in the right spot for genuine leadership.

These four questions conclude my six suggestions – to George and to everyone – for the tremendous journey into the depth of your own Self, for spiritual growth, and for the achievement of the highest potential human value. In summary, I have said: comprehend and take your religion seriously, take advantage when you can of crises, educate your conscience, use your intellectual power to think, search for the peak experiences, and answer the four questions.

Work hard enough and long enough at part or all of this advice, and I'm sure that one day a light will flash, and you'll shout, "A-ha! I *am*!"

Chapter Four

MY SELF AND RELIGION

When I was seven, I was an acolyte who wafted incense about in the church and helped the priest at mass in other ways. Before I was much older I had read all about the Fathers of the Church and the early Christian martyrs. The pious and gentle people I was living with had in their library a *History of Christian Martyrdom*. It told the stories of all the saints, the stoning and shooting of St. Stephen, the grilling of St. Lawrence, the flaying of St. Cecile – or was it another? – and the torturing of others, how they were pinched with glowing tongs and their tongues or bosoms cut off, how hot eggs were put under their shoulders or boiling oil was forced into their mouths, how their hands and feet were cut off and their bodies covered with burning pitch.

Such books are rare today, but then they were often found in pious Catholic households in Europe. Since I read everything else I came across, I read the story of martyrdom, though it was not so good for a boy of seven. Anyway, I was profoundly impressed. When anyone asked me then what I was going to be when I grew up, I replied instantly, "A martyr."

I decided to try to live like a monk and started denying myself little luxuries, as when I refused to eat some ice cream with my father the day he returned from the war.

This was what I would call my Catholic period, Catholic in the primitive sense of the Bavarian peasants among whom I lived. Later, when I studied St. Thomas of Aquinas, I met another kind of Catholicism, one in which I found the ontological expression of formal axiology.

After a year or two the monkish life palled upon me, and my interest shifted from the ethereal to the material. I went in for astronomy and other subjects of science and fancied myself becoming an agnostic. Somehow, though, it left me intellectually hungry, and when I was about 14 this nonreligious phase began merging into my Protestant period. With my brother I was baptized as a Lutheran. I learned the Augsburg Confession. I read Luther's translation of the *Bible*, and I deepened my feeling for the meaning of Jesus Christ.

It was in Denmark, when I was working for Walt Disney, that I came under the influence of the writer who, next to the Evangelist, has had more to do with the shaping of my religious life than anyone else. This was the Danish philosopher Søren Kierkegaard. At that time (about 1931) I read in Danish such of his books as *Philosophical Fragments, Either-Or, Fear and Trembling*, and *The Sickness Unto Death*. After the Second World War, when I was carrying formal axiology in my head, I made an intensive study of all his works.

As a boy I had been deeply moved by paintings of the Crucifixion and other portrayals of Jesus. I had always thought of Jesus as being by my side.

When I read Kierkegaard's conception of Jesus as "the eternal contemporary," as one who is with us as a living friend all the time, I understood very
well, I believe, what he meant. It oriented me. It confirmed, so to speak, my
religious relationship. Thus, the feeling I had always had for Jesus and what
he said blended easily and naturally with the principles of human value
which I later developed in formal axiology. Indeed, I can find precise
confirmation for those principles ln Kierkegaard's very words.

Here, then, is my own axiolgical interpretation of the *Bible* and religion
in terms of my Self and of religion. I'm quite sure that virtually the same
human values emphasized in the *Bible* have been set forth in the "Bibles"
of the world's other religions and by other great prophets and religious
leaders throughout history. I write here of Jesus and Christianity because it
is the religious tradition in which I was reared and with which most of us
in America are familiar. The Christian accepts Jesus as the Messiah, the
Savior of the world, the son of God, the Christos; the Jew does not. For him,
Jesus is another prophet. For both, however, Jesus is a great teacher, and
what he says is true. Actually, I doubt that a great many Christians accept
Jesus as the Christ; it's likely that most Christians have the Jewish view of
Jesus. To me, there is little difference in the two views. For me, Jesus is that
person who for the first time in human history articulated the nature of man's
infinity in God. He gave added emphasis to the place of man in religious
concepts.

Nearly two thousand years ago, Jesus tried to tell us about the religious
experience in human terms and its sublime importance for our true life. But
I think his parables and teachings have not been widely understood. We
repeat them to each other, but we do so without comprehension; conse-
quently, when we do try to put them into practice, we go to wild extremes.
After Jesus, Christians misunderstood his emphasis on the spiritual world.
Instead of seeing that the spiritual included the material, they opposed both
worlds to each other, regarding the material world as a Fall from God –
completely misreading Chapter 3 of Genesis – and as a sink of corruption,
a cesspool of sin, with which their spirits, their souls, should have nothing
to do.

The Church, master of the Middle Ages, had as deep a contempt for the
material world as our present age has for the spiritual world. Copernicus and
Galileo had to fear torture, and Galileo actually had to face it. Other men of
science were regarded and treated as crackpots or heretics. Hundreds were
burned at the stake. Columbus was thought mad for theorizing that the world
is round. Thus did the leaders of the Middle Ages reject the struggle of the
mind to advance.

Today many of our leaders similarly reject the struggle of the human spirit
to advance.

Jesus did not attempt to downgrade the intellectual capacities of men, but he did try to show that there is an even higher reality. "For what shall it profit a man if he shall gain the whole world, and lose his own soul?" (Mark 8:36).

Man, then, must not repeat this error of the Middle Ages; he must strive to get himself in balance by establishing, besides the values of everyday life and thought, the reality and the supreme value of the spirit, of love, and of his own dignity.

Instead of living in tunnels of fear, throwing up frantic fortifications against each other, let us live in the infinite realms of faith, developing our spiritual strength as we have our mental and material strengths. Indeed, if we are to survive we must learn to live spiritually, intrinsically. We either live eternally or not at all. We must study the map of the Self that Jesus drew for us and follow its directions.

Everything we have said so far *axiologically* has been expressed by Jesus in two great Commandments, which are found in both the New and Old Testaments: "Thou shalt love the Lord thy God with all thy heart, and with all thy soul, and with all thy mind, and with all thy strength," and "Thou shalt love thy neighbor as thyself" (Matthew 22:37-39).

Since God is within us, the first Commandment says that you must love yourself fully: intrinsically – with all your heart and soul; extrinsically – with all your strength; systemically – with all your mind. When you do this you not only live your Self, you love your Self (not selfishly but in the sense of knowing and respecting and liking your Self). And the second Commandment says that once you do this, you must love your neighbor as you love yourself. For in the depth of the Self at the vertex of the infinite cone of our being, we find not only ourselves, but also our fellow man – and God. There is unity of all men in God. It is a community not in space and time, a community that Jesus calls the Kingdom of God.

Anyone may enter; anyone may join; each of us has – and is – the key to the Kingdom – the loving or liking of our own Selves. For unless you like your Self you cannot like anybody else. Unless you feel that you are important, nothing can be important to you. You must make yourself worthy of yourself to be worthy of your fellowman and of God. If you don't take yourself seriously, if you take yourself as an accident that might just as well not have happened, then you are lost; you cannot fulfill the meaning of your life.

Remember, for example, the tragic story of a girl who was called a symbol of sex but who actually was a symbol for the spiritual poverty of our day. Marilyn Monroe was a lovely and lovable woman – but with a tragic flaw in her Self. She always had, she said, a feeling deep down that she was cheating someone, that she was not genuine. She tried desperately to overcome this feeling, and perhaps she would have made it had she not fallen victim to one of her depressive spells. For her conscience and her consciousness were more sensitive than those of most other people in her predicament. She tried desperately to love herself and to love others. Love was showered upon her but she was unable to respond fully. It was no accident, I believe, that this woman became a symbol for our time. We gain the world and yet lose our soul. We give ourselves to soul-substitutes, from corporations to status symbols to fatherlands, and occasionally to psychoanalysis, and we die alone. We could also die by our own hands, as Marilyn Monroe did, in national suicide.

We lack the religious experience as an experience of the Self. We do not comprehend the Kingdom of God within us.

Unfortunately, what Jesus told us about the Kingdom of God has come down to us in a book which, I am afraid, few have learned to read and comprehend. This is because it is not written in ordinary language. The *Bible* deals with the infinite and, as we have seen, in infinity the part equals the whole, nothing is ever lost, and anything that happens is enrichment.

This means that events of and within infinity cannot be understood by the logic of the finite nor be expressed by the language of the finite. The *Bible*, therefore, uses the logic of the infinite and expresses it in the language of infinity. The language of infinity, of intrinsic value, is the language of poetry and of metaphor. A metaphor is a word of the finite language to which is given an infinite meaning. It means anything but what it does mean. For example, the word "peach," as in "a peach of an ash tray," "a peach of a girl," "a peach of a car," means anything except peach. Even when you speak of a "peach of a peach," the first "peach" does not mean what the second does. Any word of the finite language of every day can be used as a metaphor. Usually the fuller a word's meaning, the richer it is in metaphors. Take the word "rose," and look in a book of quotations to see how many things that word has been used for. Other words of systemic meaning, like swear words, have poor metaphorical use. A metaphor gives finite language infinite meaning. Metaphorical language is the language of the *Bible*.

1. Elements of the *Bible*

The four elements of the *Bible* are the World, and the three persons of the Trinity – God, Jesus Christ, and the Holy Spirit.

Axiologically speaking, the structure of the spiritual world is similar to the structure of man. Just as 'I' is the concept that pulls together into one all the infinite stages of 'me' – at birth, now, and at death – so God is the concept that pulls the infinite stages of the space-time world together and gives this world unity and self-identity.

God is infinitely good, in the moral and spiritual sense, as well as in the logical sense. God is potentially the world's Self-fulfillment. As the world becomes morally and spiritually better, it becomes more and more God-like. To the degree that the world degenerates, impoverishes, and confuses itself, it lets God down and makes a mockery of His goodness and mastery – of His sovereignty over creation. False gods and idols then assume sovereignty over man's affairs. When the world does not follow the road to its self-fulfillment, toward God, the world is alientated from itself and from God – just as a person going astray is alienated from his Self. Such Self-alienation leads to Self-destruction. The definition of the world-in-God is God's own definition of Himself: "I am I." But the world alienated from itself, that is, from God, has the definition of the schizophrenic: "I am not I." Should this definition be fulfilled, there must come the day when the world will not be.

Of all creation, only man can reach total goodness in the world, the maximum possible richness of qualities. A man who succeeds in deepening his consciousness, his awareness to an infinite depth, who encompasses within his spirit the whole world and approaches to the richness of God, such a man would be a Saint, and a Saint of Saints. This prototypal person in the *Bible* is Jesus. To those of us who aspire to Christianity, Jesus is he who came so that we may live, in the fullest sense of this word, in infinite awareness. He represents God within the world, and the world before God. He is the mediator between us and God. He must not be an historical character in space and time; the minute he becomes such we lose him and we lose Christianity. He must be outside of space and time, an intrinsic rather than an extrinsic person. (It is deeply meaningful that we keep track of time with "B.C." and "A.D." "C" itself is not in time, just as zero, between positive and negative numbers, is not itself a number.) We can understand Jesus only if we have a living relationship with him, as if he were walking at our side – the eternal contemporary. The Gospel, then, is not primarily a report of past events; it is an experience of a living reality. Too often, in organized religion, with its traditions and ritual, this experience of the living Jesus is suffocated.

The fourth element in the *Bible* – in addition to the World, God, and Jesus – is the Holy Spirit, which corresponds to the symbolic nature of man when he has made himself transparent to himself, when his Self uses his body and mind as a symbol for a higher meaning. The Holy Spirit is the Word, the Logos, not made incarnate as in Jesus, but Word, speaking of God to man. The Holy Spirit is the Comforter who would teach us anew all that Jesus said (John 14:26), the ever-continuing effort by men of good will to clarify the Gospel of Jesus, to make the World transparent as God's Word.

2. The Message of the Parables

The parables of Jesus are situations in infinity which describe for us the features of the Kingdom of God. Each parable is a metaphor. The words are those of the everyday social language and of everyday social situations; but their meaning has nothing to do with the everyday world and its situations. They mean the world of the spirit, the realm of the infinite. Once we understand this language we understand the message of the parables.

This message Jesus has put in these pithy words: "For whosoever hath, to him shall be given, and he shall have more abundance: but whosoever hath not, from him shall be taken away even that he hath" (Matthew 13:12). This is the message of the parables. What does it mean? You can't make sense out of it by using the logic of the finite. In finite language it would seem to mean that every Rockefeller is sure to enter the Kingdom of Heaven. The more money you have, the more good things you get. And the beggar – he who hath not, from him shall be taken even that he hath – appears to be doomed to go to Hell. Is that what Jesus means? Obviously not. For he says it is easier for a camel to go through the eye of a needle than for a rich man to go to Heaven (Matthew 19:24). When the rich young man asks him, "Master, I want to follow you, what shall I do?" Jesus answers, "Sell everything you have and follow me." What then does Jesus mean? What is it that one should have in order to have even more and which, lacking it, he will lose everything? It is, of course, the infinite spirit, the knowing of "the secrets of the Kingdom of Heaven." He who has the infinite spirit will have even more spirit and he shall have it in abundance. But he who has not of the spirit, what does he have? He may have much of the world's treasure, but he finds, sooner or later – as Ivan Ilych did sooner – that it really is worthless, and in the end, of course, he loses it all because he cannot take it with him. Those who have spiritual understanding will gain more and deeper understanding. Those who don't have it – seeing, they see not, and hearing, they hear not – will lose what worldly understanding and goods they have.

Every single parable illustrates this moral in one way or another. Take the parable of the vineyard (Matthew 20:1-16). Some workers put in a twelve-hour day in the vineyard under a hot sun. From time to time the vineyard master goes to the town market place and says to the men loafing around there, "Why don't you work?" They say nobody has hired them. So he hires them to work in the vineyard, and he keeps this up all day long. Even an hour before the end of the day he asks a few loafers to come in and work. When the day is over, everyone is paid a dollar – everyone, those who worked an hour, two hours, three hours, and those who worked all day. Naturally, those who worked all day protest that it isn't fair for them to get no more than the men who only worked one hour. Says the lord of the vineyard, "Didn't you get as much as you were promised?" "Yes," they say. "Well, then," he says, "what more do you want? Are you any worse off? The last shall be first, and the first last: for many are called, but few chosen."

What on earth does it mean? It does look unfair. And from the point of view of finite arithmetic, it is unfair. No business in the world is conducted this way. But this is infinity business that Jesus is talking about – this is the Kingdom of Heaven. No space or time. If there is no time, what difference does it make how long a man has worked? Everybody is there in eternity. One eternity is as eternal as another eternity, and the so-called ten-minute eternity is as eternal as the so-called twelve-hour eternity; there are neither minutes nor hours. There is no space either. If there is no space, then there is no separation, because what separates you and me is the space between us. If there is no separation, then there are no separate pockets. If there are no separate pockets, what you have everybody has. What you don't have, nobody has. So it makes no difference who gets what. The dollar that goes to anyone goes to everyone. At the bottom of our spiritual Selves we are one community. All of us are one.

The protesting workers didn't understand the logic of the infinite in which every action is plus – remember the alephs, the infinities only build up. The goodness of the Master to anyone makes all better and cannot possibly make anyone worse off. He who has received the Lord's grace will radiate his benefits to all. The last in the earthly value scale -- the children, the poor, the meek, the humble – they will be first in the Kingdom of Heaven. The first on earth – the mighty, the rich, the powerful, the important will be last in the Kingdom of Heaven. For many are called but few are chosen; few of the powerful succeed in sloughing off the lesser values of the world so that they are ready to enter the Kingdom of Heaven, the vineyard. But if they enter, they enter, no matter when. It is only the if that counts, not the when. For this reason it was possible for the bandit who was crucified with Jesus to be in Paradise with him. In that last moment he saw the whole of Life. He saw his guilt and repented; he became eternal. "Lord," he said, "remember me when thou comest into thy kingdom." This repentance lifted him to the dimension of eternity and made good for the whole of his finite sin. There is more joy in Heaven for one sinner who repenteth than for ninety-nine just men who do not need repentance.

Another parable in which the infinite meaning of finite words is transparently clear is that of the talents (Matthew 25). Before the lord goes away he gives an amount of talents to each of his servants – five to the first, two to the second, one to the third, according to their ability. The first invested his money fruitfully and became a rich man. The second wasn't quite so smart, but he did manage to increase his stake. The third, though, was afraid. He had no courage, he lacked faith, he played it safe, and he buried his money in the ground. When the lord returned, he rejoiced in the initiative and courge of the first two servants, but when the third gave him back his money, saying, "Here it is, I didn't lose a cent," the lord was angry. "You wicked and slothful servant," he said, "to outer darkness with you where there shall be weeping and gnashing of teeth." The poor servant was bewildered. He didn't know his master. He feared him because he didn't understand him. He looked at infinity from the finite point of view. So he was not saved, not lifted to the higher level of meaning, to the understanding of his infinite value. He buried his own Self in the earth and lived like a mole. The talent in the parable is our potentiality of spirit. If we do not invest it and let it grow, without hesitation and with spiritual boldness, we offend God and we actually squander our good, let it decay and degenerate. If we don't develop that which we have, we lose everything.

Here, again, reappears the theme of the parables. Unto every one who has shall be given. If we use the intrinsic, spiritual treasure within us we can only gain. But if we do not use it we shall lose all, even our earthly possessions. So it is with all the parables. Reading them with this theme in mind, you will find the revelation of a new dimension. They are the map of the realm of infinity.

Jesus' whole life is a symbol of infinity, a metaphor of the spirit. His miracles, for example, are *practical metaphors*. When he changes water into wine he changes the terrestrial into the spirit – in this metaphor water does not stand for spirit but wine does. When he awakens the dead he awakens the spiritually dead to spiritial life, when he heals the sick he heals the spiritually sick – those who have the "sickness unto death." Kierkegaard, by the way, took this title for one of his books from John 11:4, the story of Lazarus. To be physically dead is not the sickness unto death; to be spiritually dead is. To interpret a miracle we have to find the mechanics of the infinite within it. One of the most spirited interpretations is Lloyd Douglas's account of the feeding of the five thousand in *The Robe*.

'...It was growing late in the afternoon. I had been so moved by the things I had heard and seen that I had not thought of being hungry. Reuben and I, knowing there would be nothing out there to eat, had stopped at a market-booth in Capernaum and had bought some bread and cured fish. In any other kind of crowd, we would have eaten our luncheon. But now that we had begun to feel hungry, I was ashamed to eat what I had before the faces of the men about me; for, as I have said, Jesus had been talking about us all being of one family, and how we ought to share what we had with one another. I should have been willing to divide with the man next to me; but I didn't have much more than enough for myself. So – I didn't eat; nor did Reuben.'

'I daresay there were plenty of men in the crowd who faced the same dilemma,' surmised Marcellus.

'Well – the disciples were around Jesus telling him he had better dismiss the people, so they could go to the little villages and buy food. Justus told me afterward that Jesus only shook his head and told them that the people would be fed. They were much bewildered and worried. There was a small boy, sitting very close and overhearing this talk. He had a little basket, his own lunch, not very much; just enough to feed a boy. He went to Jesus with his basket and said he was willing to share what he had.'

Marcellus' eyes lighted, and he leaned forward attentively.

'Go on,' he demanded. 'This is wonderful.'

'Yes – it really was wonderful, sir. Jesus took the basket and held it up for the people to see. And then he told how the boy wanted to share his food with all of the people. And he looked up and thanked God for the little boy's gift. It was very, very quiet, sir. Then he began breaking the small loaves into bits, and the fish he tore into little shreds; and he gave these fragments to his disciples and told them to feed the people.'

'Did the crowd laugh?' asked Marcellus.

'Well – no sir. We didn't laugh, though almost everyone smiled over such a big crowd being fed on almost nothing, as you might say. As I told you, I had been ashamed to bring out the food I had, and now I was ashamed not to; so I unwrapped my bread and fish, and broke off a piece, and offered it to the man next to me.'

'Wonderful!' shouted Marcellus. 'Was he glad to get it?'

'He had some of his own...But there were plenty of people who did not have any food along with them, sir. And everyone was fed, that day! After it was over, they gathered up a dozen basketfuls of fragments, left over'

'...This is really a marvelous story, Hariph!'

'You believe it, sir?' Hariph was happily surprised.

'Indeed, I do! And I believe it was a miracle! Jesus had inspired those stingy, selfish people to be decent to one another! It takes a truly great man to make one harmonious family out of a crowd like that.[7]

Jesus, Douglas shows us, is not concerned with miracles in space and time; *he is concerned with miracles in the inner Self.*

The Gospel seeks to make very clear the differences between the finite and the infinite, between social and metaphorical language, between the extrinsic and intrinsic. Take the conversaion between Jesus and Nicodemus. Jesus tells him, "Unless a man be born again he cannot see the Kingdom of

God." Nicodemus answers, "How can a man be born when he is old? Can he enter the second time into his mother's womb?" (John 3:3-4). Jesus of course uses the word "born" metaphorically; he means spiritual birth. The flesh and the spirit, the social and the moral individual, have entirely different dimensions; in our axiological terminology, they are those of extrinsic and intrinsic value, respectively. "Birth" in one dimension is entirely different from "birth" in the other. That which is born of the flesh is flesh; and that which is born of the Spirit is spirit." (John 3:6.) This difference is echoed by a modern philosopher, Nicholas Berdyaev, in *Slavery and Freedom*.

Personality is not a biological or a psychological phenomenon, but an ethical and spiritual one. The individual is closely linked with the material world. He is brought to birth by the generic process... Personality is not born of the family and the cosmic process, not born of a father and mother, but emanates from God; it makes its appearance from another world.

This means that while the individual is of the extrinsic world, the personality is of the intrinsic world. This intrinsic world is infinitely richer than the extrinsic world and therefore, says Berdyaev, "The entire world is nothing in comparison with human personality, with the unique person of man." The same thought has been expressed by Pico, Pascal, Bergson, and others: quantitatively man is a minute particle in the universe; qualitatively he incomparably exceeds the universe.

The Gospel juxtaposes the two kinds of values – extrinsic and intrinsic – most explicitly in the conversation between Jesus and the woman of Samaria (John 4:7-39). It begins:

There cometh a woman of Samaria to draw water: Jesus saith unto her, 'Give me to drink.' (For his disciples were gone away into the city to buy meat.) Then saith the woman of Samaria unto him, 'How is it that thou, being a Jew, asketh drink of me, which am a woman of Samaria? for the Jews have no dealing with the Samaritans.'

"Jesus saith unto her" – already this is an act of intrinsic valuation. Usually, Samaritans are not spoken to by Jews; the individual Samaritan is never valued as a person but only as a member of the class of Samaritans. But Jesus speaks to the woman, not as a Samaritan but as a woman, and, indeed, as this particular woman, as becomes clear later. He speaks to her in everyday language, but metaphorically: "Give me to drink."

The woman answers correctly to the act of intrinsic valuation, but not to the intrinsic language. "How is it that thou being a Jew, asketh drink of me, which am a woman of Samaria?" Jesus answers by showing her the intrinsic meaning of what he said: "If thou knewest the gift of God, and who it is that saith to thee, Give me to drink; thou wouldest have asked of Him, and He would have given thee living water."

Both he and the woman are in the realm of value, and she could have asked of him as well as he of her. The water he wants in communion with her is not empirical water but living spirit. She does not understand and applies the language of the world to his metaphor: "Sir, thou hast nothing to draw with, and the well is deep..." Jesus continues to make clear the two kinds of value: "Whosoever drinketh of this water shall thirst again: but whosoever drinketh of the water that I shall give him shall never thirst." Thirst is of the body, of the empirical world, where there is space and time and hence subtraction and longing for satisfaction. In the Kingdom of God there is no space and time, no subtraction; everything is added unto us, and all are in creative unity: "The water that I shall give him shall be in him a well of water springing up into everlasting life."

The woman begins to understand vaguely. She asks for this water. Jesus counters by drawing attention to her own life situation. "Go, call thy husband and come hither." To have a husband and love him is intrinsic value and belongs to the realm of the living water. But the woman said, "I have no husband." In fact she has had five 'husbands,' and Jesus brings home to her the difference between extrinsic and intrinsic valuation. Husband is an intrinsic term and refers to one and only one in a lifetime. "And he whom thou now hast is not thy husband; in that saidst thou truly."

The woman begins really to understand, but she understands in her own way. The man who speaks intrinsic value is something outside her own world, and all she knows of such a man is that he is a prophet. The prophet worships at a certain place and time. But Jesus makes clear that God is not of this world but within us and may be worshiped within us anywhere, any time:

> But the hour cometh and now is, when the true worshipers shall worship the Father in spirit and in truth: for the Father seeketh such to worship Him. God is a Spirit: and they that worship Him must worship Him in spirit and in truth.

Now the woman divines the whole truth; she calls him the Messiah. At this moment the disciples return from the city, and now the conversation is repeated in a different key. One of the disciples asks him to eat, and Jesus repeats the metaphorical game: "I have meat to eat that ye know not of." The disciples, like the woman, mistake the meaning: "Hath any man brought him aught to eat?" And now Jesus makes his whole meaning clear, using not only the metaphor of meat but of anything that grows and is created – seed, harvest, fruit, wages – recurring metaphors of the parables.

With respect to understanding the *Bible* we are a little like Nicodemus, the woman of Samaria, and the disciples at the start of their apostolic careers in their understanding of Jesus. We take the *Bible* literally as they took Jesus literally, and thus don't understand – seeing we see not, hearing we hear not. Our spiritual development is still rather embryonic.

There is in the Gospel another more subtle and more fundamental juxtaposition of the finite and the infinite, not in language but in substance – the juxtaposition of good and evil. Jesus' sayings about good and evil seem as puzzling as his other "secrets of the Kingdom of God." They have not been understood, much to the detriment of the world. Jesus states the relation between good and evil in what might be called a third great commandment: "Resist not Evil" (Matthew 5:39), or, in Paul's words, "Overcome evil with good" (Romans 12:21). Jesus gives some curious examples in explaining the meaning of this commandment: "Whosoever shall smite thee on thy right cheek, turn to him the other also" (Matthew 5:39). I once heard a sermon in which the preacher said, "The way Jesus meant this is that when someone slaps you on one cheek turn to him the other cheek to see how he did it, and slap him back." This is not Jesus' meaning. He meant what he said: offer the other cheek also to be smitten. This, Jesus implies, will take the wind out of the sail of the other's anger, for there is no greater incentive for evil-doing than resistance to it. When you don't resist evil, you drain the fun from it. Nothing is more disconcerting to a ruffian than politeness. And do you know what a dog does when he is in danger and is smaller than his enemy? He lies down, all four legs up, and the aggressor does nothing.

Here are more of Jesus' examples: "If any man will sue thee at the law, and take thy coat, let him have thy cloak also. And whosoever shall compel thee to go a mile, go with him twain" (Matthew 5:40-41).

What does it all mean?

It means we should overcome the finite by the infinite, the logic of finite thinking by the logic of infinite thinking. We should lift what is evil up to a higher level of meaning. We should save the evildoer by showing him, by our example, the spirit of the Kingdom of God. How can it be done? Simply, if you know how. Take Abraham Lincoln. When somebody reproached him, saying, "Why are you so kind to your enemies? Why don't you annihilate them?" Lincoln said, "Don't I annihilate my enemies by making friends of them?" An *Esquire* cartoon showed two cavemen in their bear skins, leaning on their big clubs, and looking on in amazement at a third caveman, grinning happily, bouncing along with a little bouquet of flowers in his hand. The caption: "Boys, I've revolutionized love." Instead of bashing in the heads of his rivals, he won the heart of the girl.

Another example: the philosopher Immanuel Kant, a little guy only five feet tall, was out walking one day when there came toward him a fellow six feet tall, a butcher with an apron and a big knife, ready to slaughter the little philosopher. Kant looked up at him, smiled, and said, "Oh my dear man, butchering day is Thursday, and today is Monday." "Oh, excuse me," the man said.

What is the secret? You have to find a logic that is different from that of the evildoer but which embraces both him and you. Since his logic is of the finite – where he is on one side and you are on the other – the surest way is to insert the logic of the infinite into the situation. This will embrace you and him on the same level, lifting him to yours. It will let him save face and make him understand you, though in his own, sometimes curious way.

The capacity to use this kind of logic seems to be inborn in some people. Take my boy, for instance. My brother and I once planned to meet for an outing at Niagara Falls with our families. My brother's boy was then about 11 and my boy about 13. My brother's boy was a wild guy. Mine was mild – he wouldn't hurt a fly. I said to my brother, apprehensively, "You know your boy; you know my boy. Before you know it there'll be a fight and maybe my boy will be thrown into Niagara." "Well," said my brother, "I've thought about that, but let's see what happens." So we met and we had hardly shaken hands before my brother's boy kicked my boy in the shins. My boy crouched, hopped along on the other leg, and cried, "Ouch, I'm wounded." Immediately, the aggressor put his arm around my boy's shoulders and said, "And I'm the doctor." So they played wounded and doctor, and they had a wonderful time.

The logic of the infinite, the brotherhood of man, can be used if you know how. The most tremendous example of this that I ever heard was told me by a former member of the German embassy in Mexico City, who is now in the Foreign Office in Bonn. He was in the battle of Stalingrad. He had lost everything he had – his gun, his bayonet, his ammunition, even his coat. He jumped into a shell hole and was sitting there, shivering in the winter cold, the battle raging all around, when a huge Russian, fully armed, lunged toward him. "Suddenly I saw myself and this Russian together in the middle of nothing, and it was ridiculous," my friend told me. "When he jumped toward me, I couldn't help it; I grinned. That fellow looks at me, stops, grins, throws away his gun, puts his arm around me and by sign language we agree that whoever loses the battle will be the others prisoner." A smile took away the whole madness of war and converted the "enemy" into a fellow man.

The secret, then, is to steep oneself in the logic of the infinite. Many of us do this as a matter of course, intuitively, in a variety of situations. It is the logic followed by mothers when they defy the laws of arithmetic and love the second child and the third as much as the first, without diminishing their love for the first child. They can love a dozen children, each of them one hundred percent, for their love grows with every child. It is the logic of the teacher who gains the more he gives of his knowledge to his students, and whose greatest sorrow would be not to have others equaling him in understanding and inspiration. It is the logic practiced by the African tribe that condemns a murderer to marry the widow of the victim in order to produce a life for the one he has taken, and by the Chinese restaurant owners who were ruining each other by competition in the same street, until they found the solution. They swapped management but retained ownership -- cooperation by competition and competition by cooperation. To sum up in the words of a wit: "If someone hands you a lemon, make lemonade." In the last instance it is just plain common sense, for common sense is precisely to see the traces of the infinite in the finite world.

This is the logic, then, of overcoming evil by good. I was finally even able to reduce it to a formula which I gave to two of my students to try out in various situations to see whether it would hold water – and it did. If U and V symbolize two values – either I, E, or S – then the formula is $(U_V)_V U$; for example, $(I_S)_S I$. There you have (within parentheses) a systemic disvaluation of an intrinsic value – an inhuman use of a system – reversed, turned around, *devalued* by the intrinsic valuation of the systemic – the human use of a system. In other words the inhuman use of a system is righted by the human use of a system.

A German friend of mine who at Niagara Falls left the U.S. for a walk out on the international bridge was caught between systems. He found he could not reenter the U.S. because he did not have his passport with him, and for the same reason he could not enter Canada. Should he spend the rest of his life on the bridge? In this predicament, (I_S), the Canadians let him enter a yard into Canada and issued an expulsion order for him which met the U.S. immigration requirements, and he was able to leave the bridge. The human use of a rule of a system, (S^I), undid the inhuman use of another rule of the system, (I_S).

In general the disvaluation of a value is righted by the corresponding valuation of the disvalue. Since there are nine basic disvaluations of a value possible, namely (S_S), (S_E), (S_I), (E_S), (E_E), (E_I), (I_S), (I_E), (I_I), there are nine basic forms of the simple rule, "overcome evil by good."

There are also more complex forms, e.g. $(I_{(S E)})_{(S E)} I$. This could mean that the devaluation of a human life (I) by a gadgeteer of the nuclear bomb $(_S E)$ could be overcome by the human use (I) of this gadget $(_S E)$ – atoms for peace instead of atoms for war. Each of the many theoretical formulae of the structure $(U_V)_V U$ has an infinity of applications. The field of evil is as varied as that of good.

We need desperately to develop our sensitivity to evil, just as we need to develop our sensitivity to good, for we cannot overcome that which we don't know. So few people can smell evil, sensitively or vicariously, precisely because they have failed to develop their sense of values. The possibility of a nuclear war that would wipe out civilization is great. Yet how few people are enough aware of this tremendous evil to say or do anything about it! How few people are enough aware of the infinite, intrinsic value of human life to protest plans to eliminate it from Creation. They say, "Well, suppose we do all die. Would that be so terrible?" How few really CARE for God's creation!

A nuclear war would be the overcoming of good with evil; it would prove that man is not made in God's image but instead is, after all, a devilish creature. But I refuse to believe this is true. I assert that this is God's world, not the devil's, that man was made in God's image, not the devil's, and that the principle of good in the world outweighs the principle of bad. We speak of a nuclear war which would be the overcoming of good by evil. At the end of a nuclear war, in a devil's world, we would end not as vegetables but as atoms. Therefore, I have to say that not believing in a nuclear war I believe that man will end up closer to the angels than to atoms.

But it's still up to Adam to move up or down from the center of the world. It's still tremendously important for him to know evil when he sees it or hears it.

At the start of Hitler's rule, there were 600,000 Jews in Germany. Fewer than one-fourth saw the Nazi evil clearly enough to get out, even though they had six years to do it. The same kind of evil represented by Hitler in his contempt and hate for other people is present in the United States today. Demagogues, political opportunists, and hate hucksters are peddling the same kind of semi-violent, semi-literate, black and white, "anti" philosophy, using the same techniques of distortions, repeated lies, and malicious gossip to prey upon dull, frustrated people with no place to go and nothing constructive to do. So these victims of demagoguery go along with the mob, gulled into irrationality and madness. It is a dangerous game, one which can push a nation of 175 million people, as well as the rest of the world, into an orgy of self-destruction, all in the name of a false Americanism and a false religion. Wrote the apostle John in I John 4:20: "If a man say, 'I love God,' and hateth his brother, he is a liar: for he that loveth not his brother whom he hath seen, how can he love God whom he hath not seen?" These people, of course, do not *want* to be evil. They think they do good – as did Hitler. Somehow their values must be reversed; what they call "good" must be shown to be evil, and what they call "evil" to be good. Thus, again, evil must be overcome by good – and by love.

How does one become sensitive to evil? Well, good and evil go together. Sensitivity to one brings about sensitivity to the other. Mozart was one of the best of men morally, but he fathomed the whole evilness of a fiend like Don Giovanni. Goethe said: "There is no crime that I could not have committed." But he did not commit any; he wrote about evil in his dramas. Dostoevski vicariously lived the crimes and terrors of conscience of his creatures. Since we were not good enough, we were not bad enough to imagine all the horrors of Hitler's evilness. Because we did not, millions perished – unnecessarily.

Thus, the road to spiritual, intrinsic goals goes through moral evil or moral good, both consciously lived. Repentance is the way from evil to good, through the horrors of the soul to the depth of our own eternal being. It is a terrible road and a precarious one; but it is more certain of success than not living morally at all, but amorally, indifferently. If you have conformed all your life, have never done anything particularly bad or anything particularly good, have lived according to the rules and customs, systemically and extrinsically, you will never even know what moral depth you have. You have never developed a sensitivity for either good or evil. You are a social machine, and there cannot be much joy in Heaven for a zombie.

The fullest meaning of life comes to us only when we develop our spiritual being. If we do not develop our spirit through sensitivity to good and evil, we have limited our contribution to the universe. As a matter of fact, we all have infinitely more spiritual power than we use. The actual use of our spiritual resources, – which are inexhaustible, – is to our potential use of them about as the need of our little finger is to the living of our lives.

Obviously, the institution with the greatest opportunity and motivation to develop spiritual power in the individual, to sensitize him to good and evil, and to solve the great problem of war and peace, is organized religion. To this end, I tried to be active in church affairs. I was a Sunday School teacher. I became a lay leader of the Episcopal Church in Lake Forest. I served as chairman of the Commission on Peace and Peace Action of the International Council of Community Churches. I saw the church leading a great moral crusade to fill the spiritual void in the world and bring peace.

I must say that I, as well as many church leaders, have been sorely disappointed. Is the struggle for spiritual strength being effectively motivated and encouraged by the churches? Have they infused spiritual consciousness into everyday life – let alone the great decisions confronting us which may mean the life and death of all mankind? I believe the great impression Pope John XXIII made on all mankind was because he, with *articulate goodness*, filled the vacuum the churches had left. Alas, his work did not lead to action and, like Jesus, he left us no method to follow it up.

Our society, both East and West, is deeply materialistic, utterly unspiritual. "Spiritual," indeed, is an avoided word in many circles today. Except on Sundays, it is not considered quite *á propos*. The reality of the spirit, I feel, will have to be established by bold men who will have to risk their prestige – and perhaps their lives – to prove to mankind that there is a higher reality than that of the systemic and extrinsic levels. It disturbs me greatly that far too often today a church service is largely a social affair rather than a vital spiritual experience. Jesus remains an historical and almost legendary character. He does not live *with us*. We turn away from what he says, forgetting as quickly as we can, or neatly ducking. "He sure gave it *to them*, didn't he?" We say to our neighbor after the sermon. To them – not to us. How often do we turn the other cheek, go the extra mile, give the man our cloak? How often do we try to overcome evil by good?

We forget that we do not become Christians merely by joining or attending a church. Christianity is not a collective matter; only what happens in the individual counts. We become truly Christian, truly religious, only by discovering our own inner depth, our Self; and this is a solitary, not a group. adventure. This is a direct, individual, person-to-God experience. It is the return of the Holy Spirit, and it must return, else we remain comfortless, the two sides of our being – mind and spirit – hopelessly split.

I have been particularly disappointed that in general the church thus far has failed to become an effective influence for peace, though many church leaders have struggled to make it influential. The German parson in 1914 complimented his countrymen on the use viciously and well of their bayonets. And Hitler's armies did not lack chaplains, despite the otherwise vigorous opposition of the church. A drama by Hochhut, now playing to full houses in Germany, castigates the acquiescence of the church to Hitler.

A chaplain of the U. S. Army Air Forces at Tinian, in the Marinas, blessed the first atomic bomb mission to Hiroshima. "We shall go forward trusting in Thee," he prayed, "knowing that we are in Thy care now and forever." The mission, as you know, resulted in horrible death for one hundred thousand human beings.

Nor has the record of the church on inter-racial problems been entirely Christianlike. The image of the church as one of the most segregated institutions in the United States does much damage to Christianity – and to America throughout the world. The white churches of the South, asserts Ralph McGill, editor of the *Atlanta Constitution*, are perhaps the greatest single obstacle to racial harmony. Yet church missionaries to Africa and Asia continue to assure the natives that "God is love," that we are our brothers' keepers.

Is it irrational of me to hope for the church and its Christian members to take the lead in proclaiming the axiological truth that human life contains the supreme value in the world, that man degrades himself, surrenders his humanity – and his divinity – and insults God when he overvalues his creations and undervalues God's Creation – *life*? Our lore is full of stories of men laying down their lives for the sake of what they think or what they have or what they want; but how many have laid down what they think or have or want for the sake of their lives?

Man-made systems have ruled supremely in history and human beings have fallen their victims. All the slaughters committed legally by civilized man and nations have been committed in the name of some abstraction – some concept of nation, God, race, and now, of all things, economic systems. Always there has arisen the protest in the name of the individual, as Castellio protested when John Calvin burned Servetus for unitarian heresy, and as the *Bible* protests in the old, seldom-understood words, "Overcome evil by good."

James Baldwin, the Black writer and leader, makes the bitter but trenchant observation that the power to exterminate ourselves "seems to be the entire sum" of human achievement and that it was accomplished "in God's name... in the name of the white God." And it is true that God's Creation, which He regarded on the sixth day as good, is in imminent danger of being finished off as ultimately bad – in His name! – because the institution to which we really pledge our greatest and highest allegiance is not the church. It is the state. This is our church proxy, our spiritual proxy – yes, our Godproxy.

Nevertheless, I still have hope that the church will provide the leadership for a dynamic program to restore true religion, revive the human spirit, and resurrect the supremacy of intrinsic human values. The church is moving. What tremendous spiritual power could be generated by the churches of this country if all of them were really to concentrate Sunday after Sunday, *day after day*, month after month, upon the vital problems of human value, life, and God!

Today the church needs to address itself to something besides the horrors of hellfire beyond this world; it can – and must, I should think – deal with the problem of hydrogen hellfire right here on earth, the problem of how to keep a small fraction of the human race from dooming all humanity to extinction. It would be difficult to imagine a more difficult, more exacting, and, at the moment, less popular leadership role; yet if life is to go on, if we are to escape racial Self-destruction, it is a role that somehow must be taken.

Individually, however, we need not wait for such an organized spiritual renaissance. Intrinsic value exists as it has always existed. The *Bible* has not changed. As always, it stands ready to become a living Book for us which will enable us to link the infinity of our spirits with the infinite meaning of its sacred text.

Chapter Five

IT'S NOT TOO LATE

How do you apply value science in evaluating the international nuclear crisis?

This is a tremendous question. I think if enough people would evaluate the war-peace crisis axiologically, and could exert sufficient influence on national leaders to get them to evaluate it from the standpoint of human values, the crisis could be overcome.

The war-peace problem today carries the highest attention priority, for unless and until it is solved, other world problems cannot be solved. Man's bright hopes to end disease, hunger, and misery and to advance his dignity and worth in many other ways inevitably will be dashed. On a dead planet all human problems and strivings become senseless.

The only way I know to answer the question is in terms of my own Self-experience, my own application of value science, my own evaluation. I have been writing as a philosopher, but I see my philosophy – including formal axiology – as a means to an end. This end is freedom to live, freedom to be born again, and a prerequisite is peace – freedom from annihilation.

What follows, then, is the result of my research and study. These are my conclusions and my beliefs, reached through the application of the principles of value science to the present condition of mankind. I do not expect you to go along with me the whole way; I may go some places where you may not wish – immediately – to be seen. Nevertheless, I have been compelled by my Self to go there, come what may; I hope I shall have some company.

I shall appeal to your reasoning and to your heart. I shall put my case before you in behalf of humanity and, especially, if I may, that tiny part of humanity which is my little granddaughter. If the jury does not agree with me, or fails to reach a verdict, I'm afraid this means that my little granddaughter is condemned to death – together of course with your own children and grandchildren.

My experiences of 1914 and 1915 – the death head of the Kaiser, my father dancing off to war, the soldiers marching toward the manhole, Uncle Alex sitting on the bed crying – formed the arrow of my life. I would betray myself if I were to change the direction of that arrow.

The First World War came and went, but the mass slaughter continued to prey on my mind, and, as I said, I wrote one day in my diary that a main task of my life must be to try to find out about war and help stop it. Hitler and the Second World War came and went. I visited Germany soon afterward. Riding from the airport into Munich, I saw and smelled the stinking ruins of a people. It was physically sickening. Then, one drizzly evening, driving on the Autobahn, I picked up a hitchhiker; he was a door-to-door post card salesman, on his way home. He said that when a housewife opened the door that afternoon he had fainted because the bullet in his head started acting up.

"That bullet isn't so bad," he said, "as the one in my spine. It's terrible sometimes. When it acts up, I just can't move."

He said the bullets were imbedded so that they couldn't be removed.

"But worst of all," he said, "is the bullet in one of my kidneys. When that acts up, I'm just miserable. I have another in my shin bone, but that's not too bad."

Now here is the shocker.

"You know," he said, "when I'm lying paralyzed on the sofa at home, and I hear military music, it sends a thrill all through me, and I want to go out and march. Isn't that crazy?"

I asked him how he explained it.

"Well," he said, "I come of a long line of soldiers. They go back to the grand elector of Brandenburg in the seventeenth century. My great grandfather was a soldier, and my people fought under Frederick the Great, under Wilhelm I, under Bismarck, under Wilhelm II. It's just in my blood."

This is what I found in post-war Germany. This is why I understand well what is meant by those who say that to rearm Germany is to pass drinks around at an Alcoholics Anonymous meeting.

Thus, my postwar trip to Germany was a sobering and triggering experience. If I'm ever going to do anything about war and peace, I'd better get going, I thought. I fully realized that peace has been sought for thousands of years and sought in vain. Nevertheless, I knew I must follow my arrow. I must become one more person dedicated full time to the task of peacemaking. So, as I have written, I devoted myself to the quest for what-is-good and to laying the foundations for the organization of goodness. I have hopes that what has been started is the beginning of peace. I'm sure it can be.

Great changes in the world occur when the problem is spelled out clearly so that everyone can see what needs to be done and what he can do to get it done. I must somehow try to spell out the problem of war so that people will get this clear insight and know what to do.

The problem, I think, is wrapped up in the question "Why does a killer in war get a medal and a killer in peace get the electric chair?" My answer is that it's because killing in war is on the third level, the systemic level of value. It is part of the war system. It is "killing" rather than killing. In war you never kill a man. You "eliminate enemy forces," you "liquidate resistance," you "take the objective," you "put the enemy out of action." You are part of an abstract game. You don't even shoot. You "handle arms," and they are not yours; they belong to the United States. You are caught in the war machine as if you are the "enemy." In war the one who kills may not see or know what he's doing, or who he's doing it to. Under his uniform he's just a nice man like you or me who, without the slightest twinge of conscience, executes an order that results in death for other nice men like you or me, or our grandchildren. He's just part of the system; just doing his duty; just transporting the fire to the people. If he does his duty well he gets a medal, because that's how the system works. A killer in peace, however, is not part of a system, not an arm of the state. He acts on his own, as an individual, and as such he is subject to the moral and legal law which he has violated; so...for him the electric chair.

Why should this be so? Why do we as human beings tolerate, accept – yes, and applaud – the killing of millions of men, women, and children when it is done systemically and draw back in horror and moral outrage at the killing of one person when it is done outside that system? This is what all of us must find out and understand in our minds and hearts – as quickly as we can.

We must measure modern war against the yardstick of intrinsic human value. We must sensitize ourselves to the causes of war, recognize the motions and the signs that point away from peace. We must stop the war system before it stops us.

Already, preparations for nuclear war blunt and distort human life all over the world; they reach into outer space, they tamper with human genes, with human gonads, with creation itself. The situation is no longer a matter of politics or economics or ideology; it is a spiritual matter of life and death.

Yet it is not too late. If we despair, we despair of our own Selves. Man still holds his future in his Self, and he has been making progress. Though slowly, human unity is dawning. It becomes more and more obvious that, to survive, all men owe their greatest loyalty to each other. The fact that the history-long search for peaceful solution to conflict has crystallized in this century in such an organization as the United Nations is encouraging. I still have faith that man was made by God, that therefore he is more good than bad, and that therefore any problem – yes, even war – can be solved rationally and simply – simply in the sense that when you grasp the totality of the situation and you find the right clue, as Newton found the clue to the law of gravity when the apple fell, you have the problem solved.

Thus, the subject of value spotlights what is good and what is evil, and this is important, for you have to know very clearly what is evil when you tackle the problem of war. Here, in the precise measurement and understanding of value, I am convinced, lies our clue. With value science as a base, we can learn to understand value as we now understand that two and two make four. With that understanding can come peace and order in the value world just as the understanding of mathematics brings order in the physical world.

Human beings as individuals generally want the good, but as soon as they start thinking and acting in collective terms, i.e., in terms of a group, a mob, a race, a state, a nation, they tend to fall easy prey to evil. Since in the systemic only the system counts, all evil can be given a systemic status and thus appear justified. The legal system in particular has been used to justify evil. Remember the Remer case in Germany. The state is essentially a legal system and, like all systemic value, is amoral. It is our human will that makes the state either moral or immoral. When we condone nuclear war, we make the state immoral. We confuse frames of reference; we downgrade intrinsic (human) and upgrade systemic (non-human) values. When we venerate or worship a system, we apply an intrinsic valuation to a systemic thing, as a man does who idolizes a button or a shoe or a foot. Axiologically, this is fetishism, and it is irrational.

Let me approach our present situation from another angle to show how deeply our chaotic thinking about value has entangled us. I shall list five propositions with which I think almost everyone will agree.

1. No rational person wants to kill another rational person.
2. However, millions of rational persons have been killed by other rational persons in the name of a collectivity (a group) or a cause.
3. At this moment the tools for killing millions of rational persons are being prepared by rational persons in the name of a collectivity, i.e., the U. S., the Soviet Union, etc. (Already you might say this is rather uncivilized; individually, it is as if I were to be spending most of my time sharpening my knife to kill someone – a rather primitive occupation.)
4. Every rational person, however, hopes the tools will never be used.
5. Every rational person, then, hopes that many hundreds of billions of dollars and countless years and months and days of human time and effort will be lost, wasted, poured down a rat hole.

You may object that you don't go along with Proposition Number Three, because you don't think any rational person would rely on such an irrational policy. But the fact is that as long as you are paying your income taxes, for example, you are, even though unwittingly, going along with it, and you are not irrational. Thus, I'm afraid Proposition Number Three must stand. We cannot say that all of us are irrational; rather, as *rational* persons we are supporting an irrational policy. The reason is that our actions *within* the war system are rational, though the system itself is irrational. It is like the calculations of the engineers on the coffee break (Chapter Two). There was nothing wrong with their logic; only the logic itself was wrong. There is nothing wrong with our war logic; only the logic itself is wrong.

We are, in other words, caught up in the war system, trapped much like my Uncle Alex. As individuals, we know it's madness, but we see no way out, and we remain ensnared like flies in a spider's web.

How can we break out of the system?

We must get back from the systemic to the intrinsic. Our collective situation is much like that of a psychotic who has lost his true Self and built up an artificial self system which he desperately but unsuccessfully tries to live. I think, therefore, it might help if, like a psychotherapist probing for his patient's early thoughts and memories, I go back to the beginnings of our collective history and values.

Our history begins with Jesus. Ever since his birth we have lived "A.D.," "Anno Domini," in years of our Lord. The drama of Jesus was the drama of good, evil, and the state. It ended tragically. Jesus was crucified by the powers that were: the Jewish community and the Roman state. The law in this instance was more powerful than was goodness. As in Hitler's state, it was put to evil use. What is the law? It is the organized will of the community, but this organized will is also the state. Thus, the law is really the state, and the state is the law. This means that the state, like any system, is a human construction that is neither good nor evil but may be used for either good or evil.

In any system, and this is the important point, the state has an existence of its own, separate from those who rule it. This built-in "life" – which was later called *la raison d'etat*, the rationale of the state – is the systemic principle of the state as a *sovereign* power or *military structure. La raison d'etat* was implicit in the Roman state; it was made explicit by Machiavelli at this time of the first Italian city states in his book, *The Prince* (1513). Machiavelli was mostly a Man of Fear, who thought and taught that the world is primarily bad. He was obsessed with evil, and he made the best of it. If a prince would be the best in an evil world, he must be the worst of the bad. The world is a jungle, and the prince must be the king of the jungle. Since the state itself was unhampered by moral principles, the state was the logical instrument for the prince to use in achieving his evil ends. "If a prince wishes to keep his position, he is often obliged not to be good." Machiavelli's book was a powerful justification for sovereign evil. Nothing is easier for an ambitious young man born to power than to confuse good and evil. *The Prince* helped him to foster this confusion. Machiavelli found many examples in the Roman Empire to illustrate his doctrine. For there, he said "it was necessary to satisfy the soldiers rather than the people...because the soldiers were more powerful than the people."

As an autonomous structure, amoral and beyond good and evil, the military arm of the state, as such, has nothing to do with human aspirations and happiness, with love and family life, with the joys and sorrows, sickness and health, desires and satisfactions of private citizens – these are matters of the civil society. The civil society, as I learned in my youth in Berlin, is entirely different from the military. I can now put it axiologically: the civil society is the totality of extrinsic functions, the web of inter-relations of men in their various occupations, based on the intrinsic value of love in the family. The military society is a purely systemic construction. Therefore, in the name of the military state, good men do evil, as in the launching of nuclear warheads; in the name of the civil society bad men do good in order to achieve the rewards of society. When I speak of the military state, I mean the military bureaucracy. It is not possible, of course, without the civil society, but I do not mean the latter when I speak of the former. A well-administered civil society is still a state, but not a military state. The government without the Pentagon is still the government.

Jesus said clearly that his Gospel concerned individuals, not collectivities such as Caesar's state. "Render therefore unto Caesar the things which are Caesar's; and unto God the things that are God's" (Luke 20:25). It has not been emphasized strongly enough, I think, that what is Caesar's is merely a construction of the human mind – the state – and that what is God's is our own life. We have forgotten which side our bread is buttered on. We tend toward the tragic transposition, giving our life to Caesar, and a bit of our money and a very little of our time, if any, to God. *We have come to regard a thought construction – a systemic thing – as more important than life itself.* This is why good men can do evil and know not that they do evil. So it was in Rome and so it is today. "Father, forgive them, for they know not what they do" (Luke 23:34).

The early Christians, however, knew evil when they saw it. They well understood the evil that could arise and dominate
the state. The Christian community quietly and as a matter of course shunned war. The Church fathers – Origenes, Tertullian, Cyprian, Lactantius – made the most emphatic declarations against military participation. Reading today the records of the Roman courts on the trials of Christians, one feels transported to a long-past age when Christianity was a burning, suffering faith in the Kingdom of God. In the year 298 A.D., for example, a former centurion named Marcellus was brought before a judge named Agricolan. Marcellus was accused of "casting away his soldier's belt, testifying that he was a Christian, and speaking blasphemy against the gods and Caesar." Marcellus admitted the accusation was true. Agricolan said, "What madness possessed you to cast away the sign of your allegiance, and to speak as you did?" Marcellus answered, "There is no madness in those who fear the Lord. It is not right for a Christian, who serves the Lord Christ, to serve the cares of the world."

Marcellus was ordered put to death by the sword.

Marcellus's trial had a sequel, the record relates. When Cassian, a court reporter under Agricolan, heard the death sentence pronounced, he "vowed with an imprecation he would go no further, and threw on the ground his pen and note book." The judge leaped from the bench and demanded to know why he had thrown down his notebook. Cassian answered that Agricolan had dictated an unjust sentence, whereupon the judge ordered him cast into prison. Later that same day he was brought into court, and Agricolan sentenced him to death.

This was the stuff of which the Christian martyrs were made. When, as a child, I read their stories, perhaps I felt vaguely that here was the answer to my quest and my question to Uncle Alex: "Why do you follow the Kaiser's command?" Alas, the day of confusion of Christianity was not long in coming. It was the 28th day of October, 312 A.D., when the Roman Emperor Constantine affixed the Cross of Christ to his arms and "in his sign" conquered his competitor for the crown. It was Constantine, not Jesus, who won at Rome's Milvian bridge; the Emperor, not the Bishop of Rome; the State, not the Church. Systemic thinking won, not Christian compassion.

From that time on the Christian Church became the captive of the state, and the Gospel was used to justify the deeds of the state. Originally a faith, Christianity became a rationalization for worldly power. God became a pawn in the market place of sovereignties. The Church, for power in the world, gave up its meaning for the human heart. The great theologian Karl Barth says there began on that day "a perversion of Christianity which today is becoming more and more intolerable...Already in 314 the first occidental synod...decreed...that refusal to carry arms was punishable with the highest Church penalty, excommunication."[8]

With this "blanket authority to the state to wage war," Christianity, says Barth, betrayed its origins and doctrine, for "the normal purpose of the state, both within and outside its border, according to the Christian view, is not to take life but to preserve life."[9]

After Constantine, the Church had no martyrs who died for the Kingdom of God against the evils of their own state. On the contrary, state and Church banded together to become one great machine of torture and death for men and women of other faiths. Together they produced, through the centuries, a crop of non-conforming and non-Christian martyrs.

Today the state has grown so powerful it no longer seems to need the support of the Church to pursue its military ends.

All this age-old perversion of Christianity – more than sixteen hundred and fifty years of it now – is due to man's overvaluation of the systemic and his undervaluation of the intrinsic. As our Hebrew tradition gave us the Gospel of man's intrinsic value, so our Greek tradition gave us the philosophy of man's intellectual value. We can almost see our spiritual history as a struggle between Jesus and Aristotle. It was Aristotle who, 300 years before Christ, channeled human thought into the dangerous current in which

Christian love was to drown – the overvaluation of systems or thought patterns and the undervaluation of human life.

This was precisely the scale of values which Jesus opposed – "the sabbath was made for man and not man for the sabbath" – but which organized religion through the centuries not only did not oppose but abetted, both in the Greek-Byzantine empire and the Roman-Germanic empire out of which grew our modern nation states.

Here is the rub. The paradox of human existence and the sickness which we have suffered throughout our history can be *clearly attributed to our callousness to the intrinsic value of life coupled with our sensitivity to the systemic value of thought.* The reason, a subtle one, arises from the very rationality that has carried us so far in natural science. It is rooted in our philosophy. Man, the rational animal, values his thinking as the highest of all values. The Aristotelian God was occupied with thinking, and with thinking about his thinking, and man's highest occupation was regarded as thinking about the divine thinker thinking his thinking; *theoria*, the Aristotelian term, literally means "seeing God."

If, however, you value thinking most highly, and there is a flaw in your thinking, then you value most highly something which is faulty, and all your valuation, *all your history*, goes wrong.

I am convinced that this is exactly what has happened – *a fatal flaw has existed, and exists to this day, in man's thinking.* Value science reveals that he has not been able to think validly about the most important thing there is, the uniqueness of the individual human life. Each human life is unique, but this fact has never been accepted because of the superficial Aristotelian-conceived belief – swallowed whole by innumerable generations of philosophers – that unique things cannot possibly have anything in common.[10] Aristotle wrote that "We acquire our knowledge of all things only in so far as they contain something universal, some one and identical characteristic in common...if nothing exists apart from individual things, nothing will be intelligible." The uniqueness of the human individual has never had any respectable intellectual standing. Value science solves the Aristotelian "difficulty." Value science solves this paradox of uniqueness as it solves the Moorean paradox of goodness. The thing is unique because it has all the properties it has, but the property "having all the properties it has" is not itself one of the properties the thing is said to have. Thus, things can have uniqueness in common and yet be different, just as they can have goodness in common and yet each have its own different kind of goodness.

This failure to recognize the uniqueness of each human life has held back the development of human ethics and axiological science just as other naive, flat-world beliefs have held back progress in natural science. Uniqueness, it was thought, was intellectually inaccessible. This moral obscurantism has, as I have said, resulted *in man's valuing his faulty thinking higher than his own life.*

Once, before I married my wife, I asked her what was her aim in life. She said it was to see her grandchildren. Well, twenty-six years later we were driving from Mexico City to New York to see our first grandchild. We reached San Antonio at the height of the Russo-American confrontation over Cuba. That day, October 24, 1962, the city seemed lifeless, with only leaves whirling in the wind, as at the end of *On the Beach*. The mood was eerie and ominous. The President had taken his blockade action against Cuba, and now it was up to Khrushchev whether we would see our grandchild or not.

Here is what my wife later wrote to a friend:

> During the whole week of crisis I had the feeling that I was being played with in some cruel, willful game. I cannot describe to you my sense of frustration at being forced to consider not seeing my grandchild because of politics, at knowing that those who made those politics could tell me when to die and when to live. The senselessness of the whole thing made me furiously resentful. Yet I still cannot blame Mr. Kennedy nor, for that matter, Mr. Khrushchev. Both are caught in their systems – but so are we.

Generations throughout history have conditioned us to accept these systems. They have hung iron curtains between us and reality, the truth about their evils, so we have to make a conscious effort to penetrate those curtains to find out what we are up against.

Our present predicament did not fall ready-made from the sky. It can be said to have resulted from the combination of three man-made institutions or forces – science and the state positively, and the church negatively. Understand that none of these forces is of itself an influence for evil. Each becomes good or evil according to the use made of it. As systems, all three are amoral. There was a time when the church was the villain (*"ecrasez l'infame!"*). Today the state is forced to play the villain's role by its impersonal, anti-human, built-in military structure. Behind this shield scoundrels historically have been able to pose as heroes, all civil resources have been employed for immoral ends, and inhuman passions and perversions have raged unchecked and unpunished. Today national nuclear forces operate in the territory of humanity against the will of humanity, against society, against my grandchildren and your grandchildren.

How has this come about?

It is the result of a trilogy of tragedies. The first was the Tragedy of Rome – military despotism; the second, the Tragedy of Feudalism – military absolutism; the third, the Tragedy of Democracy – military giantism. The process is the same throughout, repeated on ever higher turns of the spiral of history: *the exploitation of the civil – with its rhythm of birth, life, love, and death – by the military state.*

1. The Tragedy of Rome

The Roman Empire was the first great Western society. It bound together an infinite manifold of climes and countries, peoples and occupations, customs and traditions with a structure of law and administration known as the *pax Romana*, the Roman peace. It safeguarded a continent of civilized and sophisticated living in an ocean of barbarian tribes whose waves were held back by walls and lines, forts and camps. The military served to protect and defend the civil society. It served this society. No troops, no military installations were seen in Italy. Augustus, after the civil war, had returned the armed forces to the frontiers, keeping them away from the centers of political power, Rome and Italy. He sought to keep civil and military administration separate and to prevent the army from interfering with political life.

For two hundred years Rome flourished in the Golden Age of Augustus. However, when Commodus took over as emperor upon the death of the philosopher-emperor, Marcus Aurelius, in 180 A.D., decay set in. There began a rule of violence and passion which elevated the military to the rule of the Empire. Eventually, it sucked the resources of the civil society into the Empire's "defense" and thus weakened what it was supposed to strengthen.

Commodus was a degenerate whose life is described by one historian as "repulsively lascivious." For thirteen years he carried on with women and boys and murdered many of the leaders of Rome, either through jealousy or greed. The Romans as a whole knew he was evil but, indifferent and afraid, did nothing. One day, however, the emperor's concubine discovered she was on the list of those to be killed, and she enlisted the aid of an athlete to strangle Commodus to death in his bath.

The damage, though, had been done. From this time on Rome was run by the military, and the empire was doomed. As the military dominated the civil society, the Roman disaster accelerated like an avalanche. One after another, Roman armies took over, made their commanders emperors, then shifted allegiance and connived to depose them in favor of new commanders. In the fifty years between 235 and 285, twenty-six emperors came and went. Only one died a natural death. They were the victims of the power system. Everything they did turned out wrong. By identifying the military power of the state with that of the state's civil functions, they plundered and exploited the civil society. They used the income of the Empire to build up the military machine beyond all practical limits and thus bankrupted the state. Exorbitant expenses weakened the texture of society. The people shelled out heavy taxes without receiving any value in return, for the military expenses were uncreative. Everyone, eventually, worked for the military state. The military took over not only the imperial, or federal, police but the whole civil service, which had consisted of the best educated and noblest families and whose chief business was the financial and economic progress of the state – the administration of its civil society. As the army became stronger, the command posts of the civil society became permeated with present and former military personnel.

What made matters worse was that the army came to represent the less civilized part of the population, men who lived outside the stream of Roman civilization. When this pool of manpower ran low, the army began to hire men from beyond the borders, especially Germans, who were the most highly prized – and priced – soldiers and had no taint of civilization. They became the guards of the Emperor and totally eclipsed the old provincial army.

The Emperor Constantine discovered that the military regime could not have everything it wanted without at the same time persuading the people that their own interests coincided with those of the military. This he did. He also put an end to the Augustinian notion that the emperor was the chief magistrate of the Roman people. He made the throne hereditary, completing the transformation of the Roman government to an oriental despotism. The emperor became officially a god, supported on one hand by the military, on the other by the Christian church. Church and military became two sides of the same coin, that of the Sovereign State. If a coin of the Roman state after Constantine had been shown to Jesus with the question, "Is it lawful to give tribute unto Caesar?" Jesus would not have been able to answer with a counter question: "Whose is this image and superscription?" For the image on the coin would be his own, and the superscription his own words! He would not have said, "Render unto Caesar the things which are Caesar's and unto God the things which are God's." Caesar had taken God's signature as his own!

The fusion of God and State persists today. In the Eastern Empire, it held good until the fall of Constantinople in 1453; beyond that in the Third Rome of the Czars, until 1917; and beyond that in the capital of the proletariat, with its new god, the dialectic process of history, its prophets Marx and Engels, and its apostles Lenin, Stalin, Khrushchev, and the Metropolitan of Moscow (who in 1942 called Stalin the nation's "divinely anointed leader"). In the West the fusion of God and State continued: first in the sacred person of Charlemagne; second, in the successive emperors of the Holy Roman Empire; third, in the absolute monarchs; fourth, in the equally divine and sovereign democracies from Robespierre's bloody worship of the Goddess of Reason to the former First Consul's, (Napoleon's), taking the Roman crown from the hands of the Pope to the U. S. Army Air Force chaplain's blessing of the Hiroshima bomb mission.

On August 17, 1955, the President of the United States issued Executive Order 10631, "Code of Conduct for Members of the United States Armed Forces." It says: "I am an American fighting man...I will trust in my God and in the United States of America." The early Christian would have been quick to notice the blasphemy. We seem to have lost the power of distinction between the infinity of God and the finiteness of the state. My father trusted in his God and the Kaiser, and his belt buckle bore the inscription *Gott mit uns* – God with us. I sometimes feel that such ingenious blasphemy is actually worse than the cynicism of Frederick the Great who said God was with the strongest battalions, or of Stalin, who pooh-poohed the Pope, asking how many divisions he had. The fusion of God and state is so strong today that it is hardly noticed; it is taken for granted as for example the four-cent stamp which propagates the "credo": "In God is our trust," and the sub-scription, "The United States of America."

All this began with Constantine. He completed the tragedy of Rome and began the tragedy of the Christian church – its career as the captive of worldly power.

When the invaders from the north drove into the Roman Empire, they found an empire which because of its exaggerated "defenses" was defenseless. The Empire was invaded not in spite of its strength but because of its weakness. The military brought about what it was supposed to avert. It confounded strengthening itself with strengthening the Empire. It ate out the civil society, as some parasites eat out the innards of their host, leaving the outer shell intact. The Empire looked as it used to, perhaps even more magnificent, but the core was rotten. The glory of the later Roman Empire even dazzled historians. It was glorious, especially Rome itself in its imperial splendor, its mammoth buildings and baths, columns and arches of triumph. But all this was facade. It was forgotten that a state is essentially a civil society. Strangely enough, this confusion of the military state with the state's civil society fooled posterity, and some historians still write as if the invasions were events independent of the decay of Rome, and the decay of Rome independent of the military exploitation of the civil society. We still do not understand the tragic results that inevitably follow the transposition of systemic and intrinsic values.

The Germans would have taken over the Empire from within even if they had not invaded it from without. They were invited into it. Thus, the Roman state culminated in and crashed under the tyranny of barbarian military despotism.

2. The Tragedy of Feudalism

In Western Europe, after the Roman Empire, society began a gradual and uninterrupted evolution from the feudal state to the nuclear state. At first, after the fall of Rome in 410 A. D., anarchy prevailed. People were beset not only by marauding bands in their own backyards but by enemies from afar – savage nomads from Siberia and China, Arabs from the South, fierce bands from the North. Mortal danger threatened on all sides. So the people, living mostly in rural areas, for the cities were destroyed, joined locally under the protection of the strongest – a Roman official, a legionnaire, a bishop, or perhaps a strong peasant. They pledged him their work and their help against the enemy, and he pledged them protection.

Thus was born the feudal system and, indirectly, the nation state. Originally, this system was beautifully adapted to its purpose: to maintain islands of order in chaos. The civil society fed the military arm and the military arm protected the civil society. There was no military state, only the protective arm of the lord who guaranteed the peace in accordance with the feudal contract. The protecting strongman fulfilled the function of a true police force. Looked at another way, the feudal contract was like an insurance policy: the strongman promised protection in case of emergency; the insured paid as premium the strongman's sustenance and promised his help in an emergency. The feudal partners formed, in effect, a mutual insurance company, and the contract was based on the need for protection against the prevailing chaos and anarchy.

This contract was legitimate and valid as long as this need existed, but when a normal society developed again – when the land was put to the plow, roads were built, cities founded, and communication grew – the old dangers gradually disappeared. There was no more wasteland for marauding bands to roam; the few criminals were kept under control by the people themselves – the peasants, burghers, and their police. The protection of the feudal lord became unnecessary, but he did not disappear. What had been the blessing of protection now became the curse of exploitation.

The lord, the baron, the knight, and other nobility that had grown up in the hundreds of years of chaos were not about to sit uselessly in their castles. Since all the former protector knew was war and warfare, he now became the robber. He swooped down, robbed the merchants, strung up those who protested, claimed the land of the people, stole from them mercilessly, and made them his serfs. He forced them into military service and increased his domain through wars with neighbor lords and barons. He perverted the original purpose of the contract, defense and protection, into aggression and destruction. Thus, huge domains were created: out of the Ile de France, a little island in the Seine, the nation of France; out of the Norman Duchy of

Normandy, England; out of the Grand Duchy of Kiev, Russia; out of the Mark of the Count of Brandenburg, the German Empire.

By a million perversions of the feudal contract arose the age of the nation states with their large armies. In the beginning a nation state was the personal preserve of an absolute prince. *Absolutism was the military perversion of feudalism.* As the need of the people for protection decreased, the appetite of the princes for power increased. They invoked again the Constantinian principle that the ruler has supreme power over his citizens and subjects, unrestrained by law and answerable only to God. The ruler became, again, as at the end of the Roman Empire, the representative of God on earth, and he arrogated to himself the right to play God.

The absolute ruler owned both the military and the civil society. The whole nation was his personal estate. He was head of a new military fiscal bureaucracy; a *fiscal* bureaucracy because he had to have money to operate, and a *military* bureaucracy because the money was used primarily for military ends. Out of this development came the absolute monarchies of Louis XIV in France, Henry VIII and Elizabeth I in England, Peter the Great in Russia, and Frederick the Great in Germany.

The citizens were allowed to enter the prince's service, to form part of the military-fiscal bureaucracies, and to share in Sovereignty itself – to mirror themselves in the splendor of its divine origin, its high purpose, and its rich material rewards. Thus the citizens could identify themselves with the naked power of the state.

As a result, my parents danced when my father was accepted in the Kaiser's army.

The prince tried to keep the military and the civil society strictly apart, and for a time this was possible. Frederick the Great, for example, was particularly proud of the smooth way in which his country functioned despite his wars. War was a military matter which was fought "in the field" and need not concern the civil society. It was a contest between dynasties, a kind of tournament, and defense and destruction were not confused. Frederick told his generals, "You are to protect my country, not to ruin it."

When countries were ruined, as in the wars of Louis XIV and later in World Wars I and II, revolutions followed. People resented the disruption of civil life brought about by military disaster. Most revolutions, however, came too late; they occurred after the powers of the dynasties had crested. The revolution against Louis XIV was made against Louis XVI; the revolution against Frederick the Great was made against Wilhelm II. This meant the dynasty had ceased to be the master of the fiscal and military bureaucracies.

These bureaucracies had by then become independent, self-perpetuating machines. Thus the revolutions were always directed against the wrong target. They ought to have been directed against these machines. Instead they were directed against the princes who by that time were nothing but figure-heads of these machines. As a result, when the prince was deposed, the machines quietly continued to function and develop ever greater power as if nothing had happened. They didn't even bother to change the label on the fiscal-military mixture. It still read "Absolute Sovereignty," even though now it was understood to belong to the People rather than the King or Emperor. The mixture in the bottle did not change, only the pharmacist did.

In the new states of popular or People's democracies, the process of feudal evolution continued until the military bureaucracy took over completely, controlling fiscal affairs and involving members of the civil society as servants or, feudalistically speaking, vassals of the power structure. So successful has this involvement been that the present-day citizen argues fallaciously, as did the subjects of the Kaiser, "My country is powerful; I am a citizen of my country; therefore, I am powerful." He feels himself personally sovereign, divinely anointed, ready to "defend his country" and, if need be, die for it. But what he defends, I'm afraid, is not his "country" but the military power that exploits it.

What I felt to be true of the Germany of my youth is still true, and even more so, of every "great power" of today.

3. The Tragedy of Democracy

The mighty bureaucratic apparatus of the military-fiscal state, created by the absolute princes, not only still rules today, it is more powerful than ever. This is the Tragedy of Democracy. It has remained untouched by all the revolutions. Napoleon took over and built upon the military machine of the Republic, which in turn had taken over the military apparatus of the monarch and greatly expanded it by the invention of universal military service. Hitler took over the military machine from the hands of the Republic and built it into the monster of World War II, as the Republic had taken it over from the Empire and the Empire from the King of Prussia. Lenin and Trotsky and their comrades took over what was left of the military apparatus of the Czars; within three years of 1917 the "revolutionary" army contained 50,000 commissioned and 250,000 non-commissioned former Czarist officers who, in their turn, became comrades.

Neither the German nor the Russian nor the American nor, for that matter, the French, the English, the Indian, the Chinese, or any other revolution has challenged the supremacy of the state's military power over the life and death of its citizens. Revolutions so far have meant nothing but the transition of sovereign power from owners to managers. The machine grinds on not, as before, at the ruler's command, but "with the consent of the governed."

It infiltrates today's political institutions. Juridical safeguards such as separation of powers, bills of rights, guarantees of individual freedom, civil liberties, and the like scratch the surface but do not change the core. Every constitution contains an emergency trap door through which the rights, the freedoms, and the liberties of the individual can disappear.

Strangely enough, these very rights and liberties come to justify, ideologically, the slaughters of the revolutions and the subsequent "just" wars of the republics. What was done before for the glory of the King is now done for the glory of the People – for Liberty, for Freedom, for Brotherhood. These human ideals join others, including the ideal of Christian love, which at various times have been used to justify murders, massacres, and wars.

The United States of America began predominantly as a civil society, with an insistent warning from George Washington "never to run the course which has hitherto marked the Destiny of Nations" and permit its military function to become dominant. Yet even the United States has been drawn into the maelstrom of the feudal power apparatus and has built the most powerful, most deadly military machine in all history. Today's nation state is a feudal relic – but it rides on the wings of a jet stream.

What has followed in a straight line from Roman imperialism and medieval feudalism is not so much capitalism as nationalism – the system of nation states. It was a great error by Marx to see the development of history primarily in economic terms. It must be seen primarily in political terms. The economic was only a secondary aspect of the total pattern of feudalism. Hence nations, whether built on Marxism or capitalism, at the core are politically sovereign states and in either case, when the chips are down, the individual human life is disvalued, which means that all humanity is disvalued.

The politics of sovereignty is one grand play, and rulers of today, like the kings of yesterday, are actors who convert the world into their stage while they play God. One of three things is bound to happen: either the public will walk out, the actors will find out they are merely acting, or the theater will blow up. The notion of divine sovereignty was a hoax when assigned to the king. It is no less a hoax when assigned to the legal successor of the king – The People or The Nation.

Today chaos is artificial. The whole world is one interrelated and interdependent civil society. Peace is the natural condition of this society, but preparation for war is the business of many of the states into which it is split. In our world community the relics of past ages persist, military establishments grown huge with their states. Writing in the *Bulletin of the Atomic Scientist*, S. J. Patel points out that the world has spent more for war in the last *decade* – the 1950s – (nearly $1,200 billion) than for education since the beginning of the "age of enlightenment" three centuries ago.

Again, I remind you that it is not the civil societies which threaten each other with "overkill," but the military systems, which also threaten the existence of the civil societies. Instead of guaranteeing the peace, these military establishments threaten it – yes, threaten life. One of the most important questions of the day is whether one nation has the right to fire into the body of mankind, as it must in a nuclear war, in order to attack another nation.

In a nuclear age, conquest has become more senseless than ever. As someone has said, "May God have pity on the 'winner ' of a nuclear war." Fallout alone is bound to return to cripple the aggressor. Nuclear war, even without retaliation, is a deadly boomerang.

Today, both the United States and the Soviet Union are committing more of their resources to preparations for war than did Hitler's Germany just before the outbreak of World II. Each is suffering from military giantism or elephantiasis. Each nation has the capability of "overkilling" the other; the U. S. can "overkill" Russia more than a thousand times, Russia the U. S. more than a hundred times. In World War II, altogether, explosives equal to five million tons of TNT were used. This is just five Polaris missiles. Hitler's whole world war equals less than one percent of our Polaris fleet in explosive power, and the Polaris fleet is only a small part of our nuclear bomb stockpile. Indeed, the U. S. today could let loose a holocaust equal to 6,000 Hitlerian wars! Add to this the nuclear power of Russia, England, and France and you can see what a piker Hitler was – he was only a Tom Thumb of evil. Obviously, nuclear war is not war any more. The military, once the defensive arm of the nation, has become an intumescence, an elephantine growth threatening its own destruction. It has lost its legitimacy and become a deviation.

The ultimate contradiction in our situation is that we do not rely on our military might to deter the enemy but *on the rationality of the enemy to be deterred by our might*, as in the Cuban confrontation. We're still alive due to Khrushchev's rationality. Actually, nuclear deterrence will prove sooner or later to be a futile, dead-end policy. Neither Hitler nor Castro nor any other madman would be deterred by the most powerful "deterrence," for such madmen have what Freud calls the death wish; they would be happy to pull the whole world down into their graves. If the enemy is rational, then we need no weapons against him, for then we can deal with him rationally and reach an agreement with him. *Instead, we use irrational means in order to rely upon the enemy's rationality – a complete contradiction.* It is international politics gone mad.

This madness is profoundly immoral. We are using a scale of values in which people are lumped mechanistically with machines – so many hundreds of millions of people equal so many hundreds of missiles. We speak of mega-deaths, cadaver millions, as a technical term. To call this scale of values anti-Christian is a euphemism; it is diabolic. It is beyond both Christ and anti-Christ. It transcends all Biblical categories. Moreover, it is profoundly stupid. How can we speak of *defending* human freedom when we make precisely the motions that lead to the *extinction* of human freedom? We all know, and our leaders repeat it often, that nuclear war means total destruction. So why speak of Defense? Let us call things by their right names; whenever we hear the word *Defense* let us say *Destruction*; we then have "the Secretary of Destruction," the "Department of Destruction," the Destruction of freedom in Berlin, etc. As it has been expressed by five Catholic writers, the mere willingness to risk a war that could annihilate civilization is "a wickedness without parallel, a blasphemy against Creation."[11]

The gap between contending forces in our world – East and West, communism and capitalism, democracy and dictatorship, black and white, rich and poor – is quite small compared with the tremendous gap between those who think in terms of human values and those who think in the collective terms of non-human systems. This chasm swallows all the others. This is the danger that threatens life.

This is the madness of the military-dominated sovereign state.

Such madness can end only in disaster, just as irrationality ended in disaster for Germany. As truly as I am alive at this moment, and you with me, as truly as Hitler was wrong, as truly I tell you that the present course of the major powers is wrong and must end in disaster.

What can we do about it, you and I?

There is no quick, easy solution, but there is a solution. The good takes time; one cannot be good in a hurry. A life can be extinguished in the flick of a second, but how painstakingly must the surgeon work to replace even one torn nerve. This is why peace will not come through so-called strong men. They look for easy and fast solutions. It will come through men of patience, compassion, and humility – men of faith. I think there is a clue in Nevil Shute's *On the Beach*. When Peter Holmes and his wife Mary are about to take their cyanide pills as all life expires on the planet in the wake of nuclear war, they ask themselves if it could have been stopped.

> "I don't know," Peter says. "Some kinds of silliness you just can't stop. If a couple of hundred million people all decide that their national honor requires them to drop cobalt bombs upon their neighbor, well, there's not much that you or I can do about it. The only possible hope would have been to educate them out of their silliness."[12]

This is the clue as well as the hope. We must educate ourselves out of our silliness. We as a people are keenly aware of the dangerous situation we are in. We know we are living a nightmare. What we don't know is that this nightmare is unnecessary, that it is not reality.

I once lived through a nightmare that dissolved itself. I killed a man. I backed my car out of the driveway when, in the rear mirror, I saw a body fly through the air. I stopped, rushed out, and there, with glassy eyes and blood all over his abdomen, lay a man. I ran into the house, called the Red Cross, called the police, and rushed out again. The body was gone. A few people were standing around. "Where's the corpse?" I asked. "Guess that's me," a man answered. He was dead drunk, with glassy eyes, and a broken bottle of red wine sticking out of his trousers pocket. I went back into the house and dropped into a chair. It was like awakening from a nightmare, a nightmare of real life. I did kill a man; I went through all the horror of it emotionally and physically. But it was not true. My emotions and exhaustion were real, but the situation was unreal.

So is your situation and mine unreal, contrived, synthetic; it looks like what it is not. But though the situation from which the danger arises is artificial, the danger is real enough. We cannot awaken from it as I did by the grace of circumstance; we have to dissolve it *ourselves*.

We must educate ourselves. We must learn to measure values so that we may learn better how to recognize good and evil. No question on sovereignty can be permanently solved unless there are as definite ways for people to think about moral value as there are to think about mathematics and the natural sciences. This is why, in my opinion, so much depends upon development of an axiological science of value that can show the way to the establishment of the Sovereignty of Reason, in moral law as well as natural law.

Not only must we learn values, we must apply what we learn. We must, by words and actions, teach our fellow countrymen, our colleagues, our leaders, how to distinguish good from evil. We must show up clearly the craziness implicit in the contemplated extermination of the world's people for the sake of world supremacy.

As Americans, we have the innate capacity to end our nightmare. We are at heart a civilian people, and our civil virtues can be our salvation and mankind's. We can return to the roots of our country and make a breakthrough to a new frontier of spiritual strength. We can return to the ideas of the fathers of our country, to the morality of Christianity, and once again hear and heed the voice of Jesus. We can again give to Caesar what is Caesar's and to God what is God's – and stop giving to Caesar what is God's.

The suicidal politics pushed by the nuclear powers today, in disregard of the majority of mankind as expressed in United Nations resolutions, is possible only because the general public in these nations has not spoken. Our nation was founded for life, liberty, and the pursuit of happiness. Our present course, I'm afraid, is one of death, constriction, and the pursuit of agony. Ralph Lapp says in *Kill and Overkill*, "Never in history has the human race looked so much like sheep marching silently to slaughter." But, the author says, "The power of the individual is not negligible; it can be greater, indeed, than 30,000 megatons."[13]

James Reston points out in the New York *Times* (May 12, 1963) that "The greatest potential force for common sense in this country lies with the detached, unorganized and usually inarticulate moderates," but that when they avoid the struggle, as they usually do, when they are silent, except in their own drawing rooms, they leave the field wide open to the extremists, the propagandists, the crackpots.

Our day cries for moral leadership. We must mobilize our compassion and the intrinsic moral goodness of America to break the power chain of divine sovereignties and permit the human state to succeed the military state. For it is the moral goodness of America that makes this country great, the goodness that recognizes the infinite intrinsic value of the human person. We need to translate this moral goodness into international relations. We need to export it, for, in the long run, it – rather than our wealth, our standard of living, and our naked power – is what attracts the rest of the world to America. I have no doubt that the Soviet Union fears our goodness much more than our badness.

This is America's great opportunity to lead the world from war and death to peace and life. For, believe me, the question is not whether to be red or dead, but whether to be alive or dead, whether to be or not to be. Only when one is alive does one have the choice to be what one wants to be. It is all well and good to be free to speak and to worship, to assemble, to travel, to own property, to enjoy speedy and fair trial. But what good is all this if we are not free to breathe, free to eat, free to love, free to live. These are freedoms which are spelled out nowhere and violated everywhere. The nuclear nations have already with their fallout poisoned the air we breathe, the food we eat. They have invaded our genes, and they threaten us with destruction.

At the basis of our acquiescence in the system of death seems to be a deep desire to die, to cease to exist, to cease to struggle – a degeneration of the race.

Those who seek to pursue policies that will inevitably lead to nuclear war are throwing up the sponge, despairing of being able to beat the Russians in peace. They run away from the challenge of life and of communism and they would rather be dead than have a chance to compete with the Reds peacefully. They fear appeasement of Russia but not appeasement of Death.

They accept the ultimate peace which would reign if the world were converted into a cemetery.

Suicide is a sin, and in some countries a crime. Obviously, only those can be guilty who know what they are doing. Hence, I speak only to those who have awakened to our plight, who are aware of it, and who are resigned to it. I do not speak to those who live in the fool's paradise of their everyday pursuits, their jobs and comforts and flags. They are children, perhaps dangerous children, who play with lethal power as with marbles. If they destroy mankind, it can be said for them that they know not what they do.

But can those of us who are awake to our plight and yet do nothing about it be forgiven? We know what we are *NOT* doing. Can our paralysis of will, our torpidity of soul, our resignation to perishing be forgiven? We seem to be heroically and unimaginatively resigned to be the last generation on earth. In our own minds, we are the generation of the doomed, of those about to die. This means we have little hope for our children to grow up to live healthy and better lives. They are our amputated future. They are like dead branches that will fall off when the trees are shaken. They are promises never to be fulfilled, buds never to bear fruit.

Can this kind of defeatism be forgiven?

Then why do we succumb to it? Why don't we do what we know we should do? Largely, I think, because we do not know we *can*. We do not know our own strength. We have not reached inside to mobilize our own goodness, our own spiritual power.

It's almost as if we were among a hundred or so passengers on an intercontinental jet liner flying serenely on its way. One of the passengers takes out a big black cigar and puffs heavy smoke into the plane, almost choking the air-conditioning system. A stewardess asks him kindly to stop, but he pays no attention. She calls the Captain, who also asks him to stop, with no result. The man puffs on. Everybody is coughing.

Then another passenger lights a big black cigar and starts smoking, too. More coughing. The Captain says: "I have to order both of you to stop smoking." Finally the first smoker deigns to answer: "This is not a cigar, it is a bomb. When it has burned halfway, it will explode." Thereupon the other smoker speaks up, "Don't worry, for mine also is a bomb, and when it is half gone, it will blow up, too; and it will blow up first, because I smoke faster."

As the smoking race goes on, big black mushroom-like clouds envelop the passengers.

What should the passengers do? Well, it seems rather obvious – remove and destroy the cigars.

Let me repeat – *it is not too late*. We may be appalled and dismayed at the peril that besets us, but we ourselves have brought about that peril, and just as surely we can, if we will, dispel that peril. War is man-made; so is peace. It comes down, then, to a simple choice and to human action based upon that choice. S. J. Patel puts it so:

> There is now an accumulation of technical knowledge which in an outburst of half an hour of insanity could devastate almost all animal objects, the product of patient evolution over the ages. But if wisely utilized, it also has the potential to overcome in half a century the age-old afflictions of mankind – squalor, poverty, want, and disease. Humanity is thus being steadily pressed to choose between half an hour of insanity or half a century of farsighted international cooperation.[14]

There are some hopeful signs. Historian Arnold J. Toynbee observes that for 500 years now, the human race has been moving progressively from tribal or national organization (which he describes as "an idolatrous and disastrous form of religion") to world unity, "mankind's only alternative to mass suicide."

Faith in God and in mankind also has substance in the fact that, despite wayward currents of thought, human life remains, for rational persons, the supreme value in the world. The science of value proves this to be so. Just as natural science helps us use the strength of nature, axiological science will help us use the even greater strength of the human spirit to break out of the system that has hypnotized and enslaved us. Then we and our grandchildren will truly have freedom to live.

Though value science is still in a formative stage, I am convinced that its application *will* help us emerge from collective madness to individual rationality. It can help convert international relations into inter-human relations and enable every person, no matter what race, creed, or color, to enjoy his fellowman in his infinite intrinsic value. It can help tear down the artificial walls that systemic thinking has erected between us and make us truly human. It can help make nuclear power a servant of humanity rather than its hangman. This beautiful world must go on. It will go on if every one of us sees the reality of the situation and, with moral sensitivity to good and evil, acts accordingly.

END – 10-10-63

APPENDIX: THE FINAL YEARS

Arthur R. Ellis

Robert S. Hartman was engaged in multiple activities regarding his philosophy from 1963, when his original manuscript for *Freedom to Live* was written, until his death on September 20, 1973. He remained a Research Professor of Philosophy at the National University of Mexico, a position he went to in 1957, and served in the same capacity for six months each year at the University of Tennessee at Knoxville from 1968 until his death. He was a visiting professor in the Department of Philosophy at Yale University in 1966.

Throughout this period he continued to pursue "goodness" through the exposition and application of the principles of formal axiology. The publication of his chapter, "The Measurement of Value," in *Reason and Emotion in Psychotherapy*[15] by Albert Ellis in 1963 brought considerable attention to these ideas. His correspondence files contain many requests for reprints of this article from all over the country. His cardinal work, *The Structure of Value: Foundations of Formal Axiology*, was published in the United States in 1967, after much negotiating and editing. The original version had been published in Mexico in 1959.

A great deal of his attention was given to the development and marketing of his value test, the *Hartman Value Profile*, because he saw it as an easy and effective way to demonstrate the power of formal axiology. The test was inspired by a seminar on values with students in Professor Erich Fromm's class in psychoanalysis in about 1960. Dr. Hartman had formulated a table of values using the concepts of formal axiology which, after discussion in this seminar, brought the realization that a test of value measurement could be developed from it.

In 1965, Dr. Hartman became associated with a group in Boston for the purpose of preparing the values test for marketing. At that time the test was called *The Hartman Inventory*. Subsequently he began work on a clinical manual of interpretation which he wrote in segments over the next few years. Disagreements with the Boston group led to his establishing a new corporation in Texas in 1969 called Axiometrics, Inc. However, this situation did not work out well either, so the Axiometric Testing Service was started in Tennessee. Later, in 1973, arrangements to market the *Hartman Value Profile* were also made with Research Concepts in Muskegon, Michigan, which are still in effect.

The Hartman test of values was used extensively in Mexico by psychiatrists, researchers, the National University, and the Social Security Institute. His records show that during a twelve month period in 1968-69, 24,000 tests were administered in Mexico. Dr. Hartman hoped that the *Hartman Value Profile* would become widely used in the United States. Though it has been utilized by practitioners for clinical work and for various kinds of research, including validity and reliability studies, the HVP has not yet gained the popular use he envisioned.

Dr. Hartman always felt that the responses to the analysis of the test results, which reveal so much about an individual, was a personal validation of considerable significance. He often referred to the value profile as "an x-ray of the soul." When looking at data collectively for a particular group of people, he described the test as "a psychosocial x-ray." He believed that the value patterns revealed by the *Hartman Value Profile* could indicate the potential for certain behaviors, for example, a propensity for violence. In 1970, during the era of worldwide outbreaks of violence and rioting, he submitted a lengthy memorandum to the National Institute of Mental Health. In this memorandum he delineated the theory and background of the *Hartman Value Profile* and suggested its use on a national scale as a screening instrument to predict violent behavior, pertaining both to specific persons and to communities. Thus areas of greatest risk could be identified and the potential threat defused. A similar proposal with a different focus was submitted to the Rehabilitation Services Administration in 1971. This document included a demonstration study using the *Hartman Value Profile* results as part of the assessment process for vocational rehabilitation clients, reflecting individual strengths and weaknesses.

Dr. Hartman believed that the results the HVP generated has these kinds of widespread applications in the hands of skilled formal axiological practitioners. Although the principles of formal axiology have much broader usage, the *Hartman Value Profile* is one of the most tangible products of the theory.

During his last ten years he remained a prolific writer, reader, and correspondent. On a listing of works for 1967-68, for example, he notes twenty books and articles either completed or in progress. Later there were references to a book he planned to write, *Principia Axiometrica*, which would compile his years of thinking about value theory. However, it was not to be.

His library in Cuernavaca was a testament to his love of books. Mrs. Hartman has said that in the early days he used to buy books when they really needed the money for other things. His library contained 40,000 volumes, some of which were collector's items, and was valued at $250,000.

His correspondence dealt with many subjects and spanned the globe. He exchanged letters with other scholars in the Soviet Union, Israel, Poland, India, France, Canada, Sweden, Germany, and Austria.

Dr. Hartman chaired a section on "Ethics and the Philosophy of Values" at the Fourteenth International Congress of Philosophy in September 1968 in Vienna. At this conference he met Dr. Viktor Frankl, the founder of the theory of logotherapy. In August of 1968 he had written to Dr. Frankl inviting him to his session and sending him a copy of *The Structure of Value*. From their meeting in Vienna came a proposal from Frankl to establish with Hartman an Institute for Value Analysis and Logotherapy in the United States. Later correspondence discussed the Institute further, but the Institute never came to fruition. In the late 1960's Hartman served on the Board of Editors of the *Journal of Transpersonal Psychology* along with Frankl, Sidney M. Jourard, Abraham H. Maslow, Arthur Koestler, and Robert Tannenbaum.

World peace was ever a concern of Dr. Hartman's. In 1963 the Thirteenth International Congress of Philosophy met in Mexico City. As an apparent outgrowth of this meeting, Dr. Hartman was inspired to propose a "Peace Fund of the Non-Nuclear Nations" directed at non-aligned, non-nuclear nations. He assembled a document on this topic and sent it to countries in the United Nations. His correspondence indicates that he sent letters in 1964 about the Peace Fund to Mexico, Ghana, India, Indonesia, The United Arab Republic, Finland, Yugoslavia, Ethiopia, Poland, and Pope Paul VI. He proposed that nuclear power be under the control of the United Nations to prevent proliferation and world wide threat. Because of his efforts toward world peace, he was nominated for the Nobel Prize shortly before he died in 1973.[16]

My own memories of Robert Hartman are of the last five years of his life while he was a professor at the University of Tennessee and I was a student there. He was a person of formidable knowledge, intellectual intensity, and creative insight all of which he used assiduously in the analysis and synthesis of data regarding his theory of value. He was constantly scribbling notes on little pieces of paper (many of which are in the Hartman Collection at the Hoskins Library at U. T.), chuckling to himself about this latest revelation. Above all, he was a person of great warmth and compassion who attempted to make the intrinsic a real part of his life. His correspondence files include many letters to and from students and friends whose lives he touched in positive and uplifting ways.

Robert Hartman's legacy to us in formal Axiology is a response to the experiences of his own life. Within this theory is the foundation for a science of value, but, as he noted, it is only the foundation. The theory needs to be clarified, amplified, and enhanced. Continuation of Hartman's work is the task for those with vision to "organize the good" in the world.

ENDNOTES

1. Paul Weiss, Preface to Robert S. Hartman, *The Structure of Value: Foundations of Scientific Axiology*, (Carbondale, IL: Southern Illinois University Press, 1967), p. xvi.

2. G. K. Plochman, Foreword to *The Structure of Value*, p. xii.

3. *Deutschland Heute* [Germany Today], (Offices of Press and Information, Federal Government of Germany, 1955), pp. 153-55.

4. Giovanni Pico della Mirandola, *Oration on the Dignity of Man, The Renaissance Philosophy of Man*, Ernst Cassirer *et al.*, eds., (Chicago: 1948), pp. 228 ff.

5. S. Kierkegaard, *The Sickness Unto Death*, (Garden City: Doubleday & Co., 1954), p. 176.

6. Edward T. Chase, "Money Isn't Everything," *The Atlantic Monthly*, (April 1962).

7. Lloyd C. Douglas, *The Robe*, (Boston: Houghton Mifflin Co., 1942), pp. 261-262.

8. Karl Barth, *Dogmatik*, Vol. III/4, p. 521.

9. *Ibid.*, p. 522.

10. Aristotle, Metaphysics 999^a 24 ff.

11. Walter Stein, ed., *Nuclear Weapons - A Catholic Response*, (New York, Sheed and Ward), 1961.

12. Nevil Shute, *On the Beach*, (New York: William Morrow and Co., Inc., 1957), p. 309.

13. Ralph Lapp, *Kill and Overkill*, (New York: Basic Books, Inc., 1962).

14. Surendra J. Patel, *Bulletin of the Atomic Scientist*, (November 1962).

15. Albert Ellis, *Reason and Emotion in Psychotherapy*, (New York: Lyle Stuart, 1963).

16. Rita Hartman, "What Led to Formal Value Theory" in Rem B. Edwards and John W. Davis, eds., *Forms of Value and Valuation*, (Lanham, MD: University Press of America, 1991), pp. 6-7.

ABOUT THE EDITOR

Arthur R. Ellis, Ph.D., is a Licensed Professional Counselor who has been a clinician since 1971. He holds degrees in psychology and rehabilitation counseling from The University of Tennessee, Knoxville and a doctorate from Lasalle University. In recent years he has worked as a therapist in the Psychology Service of a Veterans Administration Medical Center. He studied axiology under Robert S. Hartman who personally trained him in the use and interpretation of the "Hartman Value Profile" (HVP). Over the years he has administered and interpreted hundreds of HVPs. His research has included explorations of the value patterns of alcoholics. He has been active in the R. S. Hartman for Formal and Applied Axiology, serving on the Board of Directors, and holding the positions of Executive Director and President. He is a certified Master Addictions Therapist and a Diplomate of the American Psychotherapy Association.

STATEMENT BY HARTMAN INSTITUTE

The Robert S. Hartman Institute recognizes that two discussions in *Freedom to Live: The Robert S. Hartman Story* might offend some people if taken out of context, but we ask for tolerance and understanding and hope that the following remarks will help.

First, on p. 19 Hartman refers to his anti-Hitler article in which he accuses "the Nazi leadership" of being "dominated by homosexuals." A young Robert Schirokauer, who later became Robert Hartman when he escaped Germany and the Nazis, published this article in 1932. It was written at a time when homosexuality was closeted and the Nazis' open practice of it was associated with their general decadence, both homosexual and heterosexual. In this context, it was reflective of the culture of degradation that the Nazis promoted. Hartman devoted the rest of his life to finding ways to organize goodness and to combat evils of all kind, especially hatred, violence, and intolerance which the Nazis exemplified.

Second, on p. 111 Hartman states that "Jesus was crucified by the powers that were: the Jewish community and the Roman state." Seen in context, this sentence is best understood to be about the "powers" or authorities in the Jewish community, not about the community as a whole. Robert S. Hartman had a Jewish father, later married a Jewish wife, Rita Emanuel, and fled Nazi Germany for his vigorous opposition to Hitler and Nazism. No Anti-Semitism was intended by his words, only an explanation that the actual "powers" or authorities who crucified Jesus were operating within the framework of existing law, which can always be used "for either good or evil," in this case for evil. It was a commentary on the dangers of power.

1. Robert and Heinrich Schirokauer with their father, Alfred
(between 1915-1917)

2. Wedding of Robert and Rita Hartman, August 30, 1936

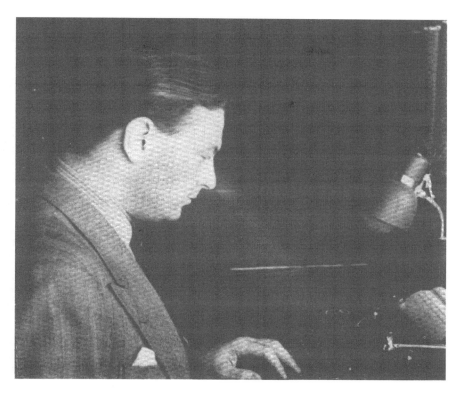

3. Dr. Harman at Work at his Desk in 1940s

4. Robert and Rita Hartman in Chicago, May 17, 1943

5. Hartman in his Library

6. Portrait of Robert S. Hartman

7. Robert, Rita, and Jan in Wooster, Ohio around 1945

8. The Hartman Family

9. Rita and Bob in Columbus, Ohio

10. Robert S. Hartman's Library in Cuernavaca, Mexico

11. Rita and Robert Hartman

8. Inscription on Hartman's Grave in Cuernavaca, Mexico

INDEX